New Directions for
Higher Education

Betsy O. Barefoot
Jillian L. Kinzie
CO-EDITORS

Critical Perspectives on Global Competition in Higher Education

Laura M. Portnoi
Sylvia S. Bagley
EDITORS

Number 168 • Winter 2014
Jossey-Bass
San Francisco

CRITICAL PERSPECTIVES ON GLOBAL COMPETITION IN HIGHER EDUCATION
Laura M. Portnoi and Sylvia S. Bagley
New Directions for Higher Education, no. 168
Betsy O. Barefoot and Jillian L. Kinzie, Co-editors

Microfilm copies of issues and articles are available in 16mm and 35mm, as well as microfiche in 105mm, through University Microfilms Inc., 300 North Zeeb Road, Ann Arbor, MI 48106-1346.

NEW DIRECTIONS FOR HIGHER EDUCATION (ISSN 0271-0560, electronic ISSN 1536-0741) is part of The Jossey-Bass Higher and Adult Education Series and is published quarterly by Wiley Subscription Services, Inc., A Wiley Company, at Jossey-Bass, One Montgomery Street, Suite 1200, San Francisco, CA 94104-4594. Periodicals Postage Paid at San Francisco, California, and at additional mailing offices. POSTMASTER: Send address changes to New Directions for Higher Education, Jossey-Bass, One Montgomery Street, Suite 1200, San Francisco, CA 94104-4594.

New Directions for Higher Education is indexed in Current Index to Journals in Education (ERIC); Higher Education Abstracts.

Individual subscription rate (in USD): $89 per year US/Can/Mex, $113 rest of world; institutional subscription rate: $335 US, $375 Can/Mex, $409 rest of world. Single copy rate: $29. Electronic only–all regions: $89 individual, $335 institutional; Print & Electronic–US: $98 individual, $402 institutional; Print & Electronic–Canada/Mexico: $98 individual, $442 institutional; Print & Electronic–Rest of World: $122 individual, $476 institutional.

Editorial correspondence should be sent to the Co-editor, Betsy O. Barefoot, Gardner Institute, Box 72, Brevard, NC 28712.

Cover design: Wiley
Cover Images: © Lava 4 images | Shutterstock

www.josseybass.com

CONTENTS

EDITORS' NOTES

The higher education sector is becoming increasingly globalized and competitive. Yet, does this drive toward global competition constitute a phenomenon—a set of significant, observable developments? We have consistently returned to this question over the past several years while studying global competition within the higher education realm. Our work began with a coedited volume entitled *Higher Education, Policy, and the Global Competition Phenomenon* (Portnoi, Rust, & Bagley, 2010/2013). Although the word "phenomenon" was central to the book's title, we realized through editing the chapters that this term does not fully encompass the nuanced manifestations of global competition in higher education.

What was clear throughout this previous volume was that "it is and it isn't" (Lingard, 2000, p. 79). In other words, global competition does exist, but not in a uniform manner. Clearly, trends toward competition abound, with global higher education rankings serving as one of the most obvious manifestations of competition in the sector. At the same time, globalization is not monolithic, and local forces mediate global trends via "vernacular," or locally determined, globalization (Appadurai, 1996; Rizvi & Lingard, 2010). Throughout our continued scholarship on global competition, we have found that governments and higher education institutions (HEIs) respond in context-specific ways and may exercise agency to resist hegemonic trends.

This nuanced understanding of the complex interplay between global and local forces within global competition in higher education is at the center of the present volume. Using a critical lens, our central purpose is to interrogate the tension between global trends toward competition and the multiple ways global competition manifests in local contexts. The chapter authors provide cutting-edge analysis of key facets of global competition in higher education while addressing important social justice concerns. The authors counter the normative approach that permeates most research on global competition—scholarship that primarily describes trends rather than questioning them or providing alternatives—and ultimately challenge the status quo by raising vital questions about social justice issues.

In Chapter 1, we set the stage for this volume by providing an overview of how globalization, the knowledge economy, neoliberalism, and other key developments have impacted the higher education sector. We analyze

NEW DIRECTIONS FOR HIGHER EDUCATION, no. 168, Winter 2014 © 2014 Wiley Periodicals, Inc.
Published online in Wiley Online Library (wileyonlinelibrary.com) • DOI: 10.1002/he.20108

trends related to global competition, including rankings and the emergence of elite research universities as the gold standard of institutional excellence. Although governments and HEIs employ several common strategies to become globally competitive, we emphasize that these must be contextualized and understood vis-à-vis local demands and realities. We also identify social justice concerns that have emerged in the face of increasing global competitiveness.

Ellen Hazelkorn addresses one of the key facets of global competition in Chapter 2—university rankings and the global reputation race. She suggests that the emergence of global rankings has profoundly impacted higher education, reflecting its transformation into a marketable commodity that may be used for geopolitical posturing. Hazelkorn posits that because rankings are viewed as independently constructed, both students and policymakers are using them to gauge excellence. This focus on rankings leads to an increasingly hierarchical system and a concentration of resources at the elite level. Hazelkorn astutely accentuates the importance of context and the wider mission of HEIs: Not all institutions are (or should be) focused on the priorities existing rankings emphasize, namely research and knowledge production.

In a closely related discussion, Robert A. Rhoads, Shuai Li, and Lauren Ilano consider the quest for building world-class universities in Chapter 3. The authors demonstrate that rankings reinforce existing hierarchies and discuss how emphasizing research leads to the elevation of elite world-class universities, shifting attention away from HEIs' public mission and social responsibility. The authors provide a compelling case for modifying ranking systems to advance a vision of world-class HEIs that incorporates social justice ideals. They suggest alternative ranking metrics that include measures such as students' social mobility, funds allocated to public good activities, and contributions to local communities.

University mergers, another key facet of global competition, are often connected to rankings and fostering world-class universities. In Chapter 4, Jussi Välimaa, Helena Aittola, and Jani Ursin examine the development of university mergers in Finland against the backdrop of global trends. Considering equality as conceived in Finland, the authors demonstrate how local entities have challenged dominant global competition trends, providing an alternate perspective that places social justice at the forefront. Although mergers have the potential for increasing hierarchies and social injustice due to concentrating resources at elite institutions, the authors document how local traditions mediated global trends in Finland's recent merger process, allowing the country's strong equality principle to prevail.

Quality assurance is a key component of ensuring excellence in a competitive higher education environment. In Chapter 5, Kevin Kinser raises pressing questions about the emergence of quality assurance mechanisms across the globe. Pointing out that quality assurance is not value neutral, his innovative analysis diverges from the normative perspective that permeates most of the literature on this topic. After mapping out the state of quality assurance and situating his analysis within international scholarship, Kinser considers several central facets of quality assurance: its purposes, its constituents, who determines the standards, and how such standards are measured. He highlights the tension between global and local priorities vis-à-vis quality assurance, arguing that attending to local customs and needs while maintaining internationally recognized standards remains a key challenge.

In Chapter 6, Taya L. Owens and Jason E. Lane explore global and local tensions in cross-border higher education (CBHE), with an emphasis on international branch campuses. They cover the context in which CBHE emerged, particularly the increasingly central role of knowledge and its importance to nations' economies and competitive edge. Providing a unique perspective within the literature on this topic, Owens and Lane analyze equity and quality issues that arise within different types of CBHE. Their cutting-edge analysis of the multifaceted interplay between global and local forces demonstrates the complexities of global competition in higher education.

International education hubs, the focus of Jane Knight's analysis in Chapter 7, are a relatively new form of CBHE. Knight considers how local actors may mediate globalization by maximizing benefits while mitigating risks. Based on her leading-edge work on this topic over the past several years, Knight provides a working definition and typology of education hubs that includes different rationales, activities, and actors. She analyzes the context of six jurisdictions that have established hubs: Qatar, the United Arab Emirates, Hong Kong, Malaysia, Singapore, and Botswana. Knight emphasizes that there is no one-size-fits-all approach to creating an education hub and examines the local needs that drive hub development in each location. She concludes that strategic collaboration is necessary to ensure that local priorities are addressed when developing and sustaining hubs.

In Chapter 8, we synthesize key themes evident across the entire volume. Taken together, the chapters provide innovative critical analysis of global competition in higher education. The authors address international literature on their topics, raise key social justice concerns, and demonstrate how local forces mediate global pressures through vernacular globalization. Discernable trends toward global competition clearly exist, yet these developments are not uniform or static.

The scholarship presented in this volume provides a platform for igniting discussions and inspiring future scholarship that considers the possibility of resistance and alternatives to the status quo. We are grateful to the authors for their diligence in working with us to open up this critical dialogue, and look forward to future conversations with readers of this volume.

Laura M. Portnoi
Sylvia S. Bagley
Editors

References

Appadurai, A. (1996). *Modernity at large: Cultural dimensions of globalization.* Minneapolis: University of Minnesota Press.

Lingard, B. (2000). It is and it isn't: Vernacular globalization, educational policy, and restructuring. In N. C. Burbles & C. A. Torres (Eds.), *Globalization and education: Critical perspectives* (pp. 79–108). New York, NY: Routledge.

Portnoi, L. M., Rust, V. D., & Bagley, S. S. (Eds.). (2010/2013). *Higher education, policy, and the global competition phenomenon.* New York, NY: Palgrave Macmillan.

Rizvi, F., & Lingard, B. (2010). *Globalizing education policy.* New York, NY: Routledge.

LAURA M. PORTNOI *is an associate professor and assistant department chair in the Advanced Studies in Education and Counseling Department at California State University, Long Beach.*

SYLVIA S. BAGLEY *is director of Teacher Leadership in the College of Education at the University of Washington.*

NEW DIRECTIONS FOR HIGHER EDUCATION • DOI: 10.1002/he

1

In this chapter, the issue editors set the stage for the chapters that follow by delineating recent developments in higher education and common strategies for creating globally competitive higher education institutions. The editors consider social justice concerns that arise with global competition and contend that contextualized priorities can and should mediate global trends.

Setting the Stage: Global Competition in Higher Education

Sylvia S. Bagley, Laura M. Portnoi

Higher education institutions (HEIs) across the world are functioning within an increasingly globalized and competitive landscape (Marginson, 2006; Portnoi, Bagley, & Rust, 2013; Slaughter & Rhoades, 2004). Globalization—a broadly used and nebulous term—has been conceptualized in numerous ways, with various scholars focusing on its social, political, cultural, and/or economic manifestations (Steger, 2013). Despite contestation regarding its definition, most scholars and observers would agree that globalization is multidimensional and that its effects have accelerated in recent decades, due in part to tremendous technological advances (Robinson, 2007). Technological progress has led to the development of a global knowledge economy, or "k-economy," with an emphasis on knowledge production and knowledge-intensive activities (Gürüz, 2008; Marginson, 2013; Rizvi, 2004).

Globalization and the rise of the k-economy have significantly impacted the higher education sector, especially when coupled with the neoliberal economic environment that prevails worldwide. With its emphasis on corporatization, privatization, accountability, and limited government intervention, neoliberalism has led to a significant shift away from the social democratic values that governed higher education previously (Chapter 2 by Hazelkorn in this volume; Rizvi & Lingard, 2010). Higher education is increasingly tied to national economic prowess in this competitive context, resulting in a host of market-driven trends within the sector, including increased privatization, strategic interaction between higher education and industry, and more managerial forms of governance. At the same time, the World Trade Organization's General Agreement on

NEW DIRECTIONS FOR HIGHER EDUCATION, no. 168, Winter 2014   © 2014 Wiley Periodicals, Inc.
Published online in Wiley Online Library (wileyonlinelibrary.com) • DOI: 10.1002/he.20109

5

Trade in Services has made higher education a tradable commodity (Shields & Edwards, 2013). Within this environment, knowledge and knowledge production have marked significance, leading both governments and HEIs to place increased emphasis on building research capacity for human capital development and national economic advancement (Rizvi & Lingard, 2010).

Global Ranking Schemes and Global University Models

The competitive higher education environment has led to a race for global stature and the emergence of several highly publicized global ranking schemes, beginning in 2003—most notably Shanghai Jiao Tong University's *Academic Ranking of World Universities* (ARWU) and the *Times Higher Education* (THE) rankings. The *Quacquarelli Symonds* (QS) *World University Rankings*, formerly joined with THE, is another key contender. Additional rankings have proliferated in recent years, as Hazelkorn discusses in Chapter 2 of this volume. These ranking mechanisms are both a result of increased competition and a driver of further competition (Portnoi & Bagley, 2011). Scholars and commentators have raised key concerns about the validity, reliability, and methods of HEI rankings, particularly due to their focus on publications in specific English-language journals (see, e.g., Marginson, 2013; Ntsohe & Letseka, 2013). Accordingly, questions arise regarding rankings' elitism and the narrow notion of what constitutes "excellence" in higher education (Bagley & Portnoi, 2012). Nonetheless, global rankings influence higher education decision making on multiple levels—including prioritization of funding and resources—thus rendering them significant to understanding developments related to global competition (Hazelkorn, 2008, Chapter 2 of this volume).

Global ranking schemes tend to valorize one particular type of HEI, resulting in a corresponding trend toward global university models of "top" players. Marginson (2006) delineated the globally focused missions, priorities, research, and interconnectivity of Global Research Universities (GRUs), critical to many nations' missions to remain key players in the global k-economy. Similarly, Mohrman, Ma, and Baker (2008) analyzed the Emerging Global Model (EGM), which encompasses global missions, increasing complexity, worldwide recruitment, international collaboration, diversified funding, increased interaction between government and industry, industry-centered roles for professors, and a prevailing emphasis on high-impact research. Clearly, global stature and research are central to these influential models of elite institutions that many other HEIs endeavor to emulate.

Common Strategies for Increasing Global Competitiveness

Governments and HEIs utilize six common strategies, separately or in combination, as they strive for global competitiveness (Portnoi & Bagley, 2011).

NEW DIRECTIONS FOR HIGHER EDUCATION • DOI: 10.1002/he

First, they may develop world-class universities similar to GRU or EGM institutions—prestigious research institutions that play a key role in creating and disseminating knowledge and producing a highly skilled global workforce (Altbach & Salmi, 2011). Governments may create world-class universities by prioritizing funds for improving a small number of preexisting elite institutions, as China has done, or by building new institutions from the ground up (Salmi, 2009). Russia, for instance, announced the goal of having at least five Russian universities placed among the top 100 global HEIs by 2020 (Vorotnikov, 2013), whereas King Abdullah University in Saudi Arabia, established in 2009, is a new institution seeking world-class status. A related strategy numerous countries employ is merging institutions to form larger, more powerful "players." A third strategy—regional alliances—involves nations or HEIs joining forces across regions to enhance their viability on the global stage (Beerkens, 2004).

A fourth key strategy nations and HEIs employ when seeking to enhance their global status is internationalization, defined as "the process of integrating international, intercultural, and global dimensions" into higher education (Knight, 2004, p. 9). A fifth strategy is cross-border offerings—including international branch campuses, joint degrees, and distance education. Finally, prioritizing the quality of higher education services by implementing or strengthening quality assurance measures designed to assess the performance of HEIs is an additional strategy for increasing global stature. Quality assurance, which may include accreditation processes, is one of the most ubiquitous tactics HEIs or nations utilize, as they may implement measures to improve service to local "consumers" and/or to enhance global competitiveness. This final strategy highlights how local priorities interact with the dominant forces of global competition.

Contextualizing Trends Toward Global Competition

Although global competition trends are evident, they are not monolithic and are consistently mediated by context-specific realities (Anderson-Levitt, 2003; Appadurai, 1996; Portnoi & Bagley, 2011; Rizvi & Lingard, 2010). Not all countries and HEIs can (or should) base their missions on existing GRU or EGM university models. Indeed, as we have found in our ongoing content analysis of over 200 national education policy documents, countries and HEIs select strategies relevant to their local contexts and adapt them to their needs.

With the exception of nations that have decentralized governments (e.g., Germany and the United States), more established countries tend to have specific, stand-alone higher education policies that include strategic priorities reflecting global competition trends. For example, the Republic of Ireland's (2011) "National Strategy for Higher Education to 2030" refers to regional and international comparisons and seeks to position the country's higher education system as a world leader in quality. Yet Ireland's policy highlights other localized priorities, including improving teaching and learning, maintaining engagement with society, and increasing offerings for a diverse population. This policy displays both dominant global competition trends and context-specific priorities.

Many developing countries, conversely, address higher education as part of a broader policy framework. Reflecting the influence of the World Bank and other donor agencies, developing and postcolonial countries' education policies—as well as those of some of the Arab States (notably Iraq, Qatar, Turkey, and Yemen)—tend to focus primarily on higher education's role in national social and economic development. In Ethiopia and Qatar, for example, a key concern is the need for higher education to contribute to national development (Federal Democratic Republic of Ethiopia, 2010; Qatar General Secretariat for Development Planning, 2011). Assuring the quality of a nation's HEIs may be critical for becoming a global competitor, but it may also signal compliance with donor objectives or attempts to gain legitimacy prior to entering the reputation race. Placement on global rankings might be a longer term goal or consideration, but it often does not play a prominent role in these countries' education policies.

Social Justice and Equity Concerns

A primary social justice concern when considering global competition in higher education is whether HEIs in all countries have a legitimate chance to compete in the zero-sum rankings "game" with established global players. Based on their postcolonial or postconflict situations, many countries are starting from a different geopolitical position; in other words, the playing field is not level. Although less established countries may be slowly improving their HEIs, dominant countries continue to improve theirs at the same time, keeping the gap between more developed and less developed countries intact.

With hundreds of HEIs striving to either place or increase their stature on numerous global rankings, the drive toward meeting externally determined criteria, with a skewed emphasis on research and elite status, has become stronger than ever. What seems to be lost in the "reputation race" (van Vught, 2008, p. 169) is a focus on other critical mandates of HEIs—such as meeting the needs of local communities and providing affordable, high-quality education to citizens. Lemann (2014) highlighted the severity of this conceptual split in the competing purposes of higher education—providing world-class higher education while also offering education to the masses. Many countries struggle to prioritize limited education resources, facing the competing goals of becoming more internationally recognized while simultaneously meeting the needs of local residents. For instance, providing funding to secure high-level faculty members—who are central to maintaining HEIs' status as world-class research universities—necessarily means that those funds will not be prioritized for broadening access. Indeed, this essential struggle to remain both locally and globally relevant appears to be endemic to the very enterprise of higher education in the 21st century.

Furthermore, the missions and aspirations of postcolonial or post-conflict nations will necessarily look different from those of industrialized nations. In countries with numerous HEIs, there is greater opportunity to attend to developing world-class institutions while also offering higher education to the masses through lower cost options. A war-torn nation like Afghanistan, however, must focus on restoring and improving the infrastructure and quality of its higher education system so that it can once again serve as a solid pillar for national development (Islamic Republic of Afghanistan Ministry of Higher Education, 2009).

The increasing dominance of market-driven measures within the higher education sector raises additional questions about social justice and equity. With specialized recruiters at top universities marketing their HEIs to international students, conflicts have emerged between meeting institutions' financial goals and addressing prospective students' needs (Redden, 2014). In addition, marketing top universities to wealthy international students perpetuates global inequalities regarding access to higher education for individuals within and between countries. Ultimately, such tactics highlight the fact that managing HEIs and systems from a market-driven perspective may compromise other equity-driven goals and priorities.

Conclusion: Challenging the Competitive Higher Education Environment

Although global competition appears to be firmly entrenched in the higher education sector, we contend that local forces can and will continue to mediate dominant trends and strategies. In a recent commentary for *University World News*, Marginson (2014) noted that Western hegemony in higher education will not last forever and highlighted the need to understand the local histories, cultural norms, and dominant languages of other education systems. Focusing on local realities and needs may not fully address the social justice concerns we have raised, which are indicative of the broader neoliberal environment. Nevertheless, contextualized responses allow countries and HEIs to define excellence on their own terms and provide other countries and HEIs with a wider perspective on alternatives to the status quo. We remain convinced that the competitive, hierarchical nature of higher education and the resulting drive toward global competition can and should be challenged.

References

Altbach, P., & Salmi, J. (2011). *The road to academic excellence: The making of world-class research universities*. Washington, DC: The World Bank.

NEW DIRECTIONS FOR HIGHER EDUCATION • DOI: 10.1002/he

Anderson-Levitt, K. (Ed.). (2003). *Local meanings, global schooling: Anthropology and world culture theory.* New York, NY: Palgrave Macmillan.

Appadurai, A. (1996). *Modernity at large: Cultural dimensions of globalization.* Minneapolis: University of Minnesota Press.

Bagley, S. S., & Portnoi, L. M. (2012, September). Expanding the notion of "world-class" higher education institutions. *CIES Perspectives, 159,* 1–2.

Beerkens, E. (2004, September). *Global opportunities and institutional embeddedness: Higher education consortia in Europe and Southeast Asia.* Paper presented at the meeting of the Consortium of Higher Education Researchers, Enschede, the Netherlands. Retrieved from http://www.beerkens.info/files/Beerkens%20CHER%20Conference.pdf

Federal Democratic Republic of Ethiopia. (2010). *Growth and transformation plan: 2010/2011–2014/2015.* Retrieved from http://www.bowrd.gov.et/en/about-us/growth-and-transformation-plan.pdf

Gürüz, K. (2008). *Higher education and international student mobility in the global knowledge economy.* Albany: State University of New York Press.

Hazelkorn, E. (2008). Learning to live with league tables and ranking: The experience of institutional leaders. *Higher Education Policy, 21*(2), 193–215.

Islamic Republic of Afghanistan Ministry of Higher Education. (2009). *National higher education strategic plan: 2010–2014.* Retrieved from http://www.mohe.gov.af/?lang=en&p=plan

Knight, J. (2004). Internationalization remodeled: Rationales, strategies, and approaches. *Journal for Studies in International Education, 8*(1), 5–31.

Lemann, N. (2014, April 28). The soul of the research university. *Chronicle of Higher Education.* Retrieved from http://chronicle.com/article/The-Soul-of-the-Research/146155/

Marginson, S. (2006). Dynamics of national and global competition in higher education. *Higher Education, 52*(3–4), 1–39.

Marginson, S. (2013). Global comparisons and the university knowledge economy. In L. M. Portnoi, V. D. Rust, & S. S. Bagley (Eds.), *Higher education, policy, and the global competition phenomenon* (pp. 29–42). New York, NY: Palgrave Macmillan.

Marginson, S. (2014, March 28). The west's global HE hegemony: Nothing lasts forever. *University World News.* Retrieved from http://www.universityworldnews.com/article.php?story=20140326123556985

Mohrman, K., Ma, W., & Baker, D. (2008). The research university in transition: The emerging global model. *Higher Education Policy, 21*(1), 5–27.

Ntsohe, I., & Letseka, M. (2013). Quality assurance and global competitiveness in higher education. In L. M. Portnoi, V. D. Rust, & S. S. Bagley (Eds.), *Higher education, policy, and the global competition phenomenon* (pp. 59–72). New York, NY: Palgrave Macmillan.

Portnoi, L. M., & Bagley, S. S. (2011). Global competition in higher education: Strategies in a glonacal context. *World Studies in Education, 12*(2), 5–33.

Portnoi, L. M., Bagley, S. S., & Rust, V. D. (2013). Mapping the terrain: The global competition phenomenon in higher education. In L. M. Portnoi, V. D. Rust, & S. S. Bagley (Eds.), *Higher education, policy, and the global competition phenomenon* (pp. 1–14). New York, NY: Palgrave Macmillan.

Qatar General Secretariat for Development Planning. (2011). *Qatar national development strategy 2011–2016: Towards Qatar national vision 2030.* Retrieved from http://www.gsdp.gov.qa/gsdp_vision/docs/NDS_EN.pdf

Redden, E. (2014). Paying a premium. *Globalization of higher education* (pp. 7–9). Washington, DC: Inside Higher Ed. Retrieved from http://www.insidehighered.com/quicktakes/2014/03/25/globalization-higher-education-new-compilation

Republic of Ireland. (2011). *National strategy for higher education to 2030.* Retrieved from http://www.hea.ie/en/policy/national-strategy

2002), as well as the changing economic fortunes of the world's power regions. Heretofore, higher education had been considered, along with health and social welfare, as a social expenditure largely disconnected from other policy considerations. The realization that in the 21st century wealth creation was dependent upon the production of higher valued goods and services innovated by talent changed this perception (Santiago, Tremblay, Basri, & Arnal, 2008). As the principal provider of human capital through education and training, as well as the primary source of new knowledge, higher education and university-based research were catapulted to the center of policymaking in a dramatic new way.

However, at a time when the new economy is dependent upon highly educated graduates, many developed countries are coming under demographic pressure. The graying of their populations and retirement of professionals, combined with the end of the "baby boomer" bubble and postponement of childbirth, have challenged national strategies based upon growing knowledge-intensive industries and intensified competition for mobile investment and talent. The global financial crisis that began in 2008 simply accelerated the speed of this change, drawing attention to the fragility of developed economies and bringing the BRICS countries (Brazil, Russia, India, China, and South Africa) firmly into the competitive spotlight. Imbalances in public and private debt and investment in higher education and research exposed a widening gap in "world-classness" between countries and regions. These factors help explain why the performance and quality of higher education have become such a major policy issue and matter of public concern.

First developed in the United States between 1910 and the 1950s, national rankings assessed the "scientific strength" of leading universities according to faculty research reputation (Webster, 1986). But it was the popularization of college rankings by USNWR in 1983 that transformed them into a commodity for students eager to take advantage of massification and those aspiring to join the middle class. Media organizations in other countries followed suit, producing their own "league tables" of universities, using an analogy to displaying sports team statistics (Tight, 2000). The arrival of the ARWU global rankings two decades later was a significant game changer on an international scale. In 2003, Shanghai Jiao Tong University was not well known outside China; however, the Chinese government had identified it for special investment in 1998, along with other universities, as part of the "985 Project" to build world-class universities. As a consequence, a group of university planners developed a ranking system in order to assess the gap between China's ambitions and the performance of Chinese universities under Nian Cai Liu's leadership. No one could have predicted that those rankings would provoke such a reaction across the globe.

Within a year Webometrics (2003) and the Times Higher Education (THE)/Quacquarelli Sydmonds (QS) World University Rankings (2004) followed, the latter of which split into two separate systems in 2009.

Policymakers across Europe in particular responded immediately, aghast that too few of their universities were listed among the world's top 100. A year later, in 2005, the German government launched the *Exzellenzinitiative* (Initiative for Excellence), followed by a report by the French Senate arguing that its researchers were disadvantaged in favor of English-speaking institutions. In 2008, the French Presidency of the European Union organized a conference championing a new European ranking system. Today, there are 10 major global rankings, of which *ARWU*, *THE*, and *QS* are the most well known. The aforementioned European Union's *U-Multirank* was launched in 2014. There are also many national as well as discipline-specific and geographically specific rankings.

Based on an ordinal listing of colleges and universities, and using a limited set of indicators, rankings provide an overview of university performance in a simple way, and are therefore the tool of choice for a wide range of stakeholders. Most significantly, by placing HEIs within a wider international and comparative framework, global rankings highlight the fact that higher education plays a vital role in creating competitive advantage, and, further, that national prominence is no longer sufficient. The results mirror and have provoked a worldwide shift in relations between HEIs and their nations. Areas of friction concern governance and autonomy, transparency and accountability, performance and productivity, quality and accreditation, and value for money and return on investment (Ferlie, Musselin, & Andresani, 2008). Governments seek to answer the question, "How can our university/nation perform better?" (Marginson, 2009, p. 591). For middle-income and developing countries, global rankings draw attention to the importance of investing in higher education to "participate effectively in the global knowledge network on an equal basis with the top academic institutions in the world" (Altbach & Salmi, 2011, p. 1); for developed countries, they have exposed vulnerabilities around reputation and status.

The United States has been largely immune to the global ranking phenomenon due to a combination of historic dominance (both economically and educationally) and complacency. In the interim, Asian societies, most notably China, have improved in both the number of universities and their position in global rankings, as a result of government investment strategies and changes in ranking methodology; meanwhile, South American, Middle Eastern, and African universities are still barely visible on the rankings (Hazelkorn, 2014a). When measured against population size or gross domestic product (GDP), smaller countries, notably Hong Kong and Singapore, do particularly well. These trends have sharpened in recent years, illustrating the increasingly multipolar dimension of the world order and international division of knowledge (Flick & Convoco Foundation, 2011; Jöns & Hoyler, 2013). By successfully linking the attractiveness of nations and world regions with the talent-catching and knowledge-producing capacity of HEIs, global rankings have become a powerful lens through which to view these developments. Accordingly, they have assumed a commanding

NEW DIRECTIONS FOR HIGHER EDUCATION • DOI: 10.1002/he

role in influencing national policy and institutional decision making. This explains why global rankings have taken on such significance at a geopolitical level.

Theorizing Rankings

Over the past decade, there has been exponential growth in articles, books, chapters, and news commentary on and about rankings. Much of this literature has focused on methodological shortcomings, often questioning and challenging the basis by which the indicators have been chosen, the weightings assigned, and the statistical methodologies utilized. Another body of work seeks to explain why rankings have become influential and impactful. In this section, I discuss this latter set of literature under three broad headings: globalization and networks of power; organizational behavior and change; and social capital and positional goods (see Hazelkorn, 2011, pp. 12–22, for greater detail). Each of these arguments independently offers a persuasive account of the reasons rankings have become so influential, but together they provide a compelling narrative and contextualization for the remainder of this chapter.

Globalization and Networks of Power. According to Castells (1996), competitiveness is dependent upon the capacity of "national and supranational institutions to steer the growth strategy of those countries or areas under their jurisdiction including the creation of competitive advantage" (p. 105). National strategies have had major consequences for higher education, and have been responsible for transforming it into a key instrument of economic development. Accordingly, higher education has become a beacon for mobile investment and talent and is fundamental for building strategies for competitive advantage. By redirecting education toward wealth creation and economic competitiveness, the distinction between knowledge and commodity collapses, and "knowledge becomes commodity" (Slaughter & Leslie, 1997, p. 38). In a globally competitive market, nations compete on the basis of innovation, which is "fundamentally stored in human brains" (Castells, 1996, p. 95), thus heightening the value of talent. The world economy is a "relational landscape" (Marginson & van der Wende, 2007, p. 15), whereby nations and HEIs are constantly measured against each other according to indicators of global capacity and potential in which comparative and competitive advantages come into play. Rankings are viewed as a simple yet powerful tool to measure performance.

Organizational Behavior and Change. Foucault (1977) and Gramsci (1971), in complementary ways, considered how power and control have shifted from punishment to more abstract forms of "disciplinary technology" that normalize behavior by regulating the space, time, or activity of people's lives. Whereas Foucault wrote about the "disciplinary society," Gramsci's "hegemony" involved power exercised opaquely through cultural norms (i.e., views, practices, and institutions), which become pervasive and are thus seen to be normalized, as "lived experience" or "common sense" (p. 419). In this way, rankings can change perceptions of education, through coercive and seductive means, resulting in an obsessive form of control that is internalized (Sauder & Espeland, 2009). Leaders within higher education often feel under pressure to conform to a particular norm or model of higher education. Accordingly, HEIs have made changes, adopted new policies, or manipulated data in order to more positively affect their positions on the rankings. Given the importance with which key stakeholders view rankings, the above reactions from HEIs are rational (Becker, 1993). Essentially, this is an argument about rankings as soft power—in other words, having an influence, which is persuasive rather than coercive (Lo, 2011).

Social Capital and Positional Goods. Bourdieu (1986) differentiated between three kinds of capital: economic, cultural, and social. Social capital is a function of power relations whereby individuals seek to advance their interests and social position via the actual or potential resources that are linked to possession or membership of a durable network that accrues certain benefits. Because only a few people can benefit at any one time, access to scarce goods and facilities elevates their premium value. Hirsch (1997), Winston (2000), and Frank (2001) argued that because of their limited nature, striving for university prestige creates a resource-intensive arms race in which the "winner takes all." It is viewed as a zero-sum game— some people gain, others must lose out. Thus, because only 100 universities can be in the top 100, rankings have heightened the value of elite institutions and their host nations. Their reputational value has become a valuable commodity for students, nations, and employers in the search for talent to drive economic growth and recovery.

Responding to Rankings

Global rankings can bring tangible benefits to a country, city, or region by magnifying its attraction and status as a knowledge hub. This is due to the convincing way rankings tell a story about the quality, capacity, and capability of HEIs and their host nations. Inclusion of even one HEI in a ranking can grant national and international visibility and help build reputation, especially for emerging economies and lower ranked institutions. These factors have helped expand the range of users beyond students and their parents to include policymakers, employers, foundations and benefactors, potential collaborators and partners, alumni, other HEIs, and many other stakeholders. High-achieving students, especially international graduate students, use rankings to shortlist their university choices; business, industry, and philanthropists use rankings to influence investment decisions, partnerships, and employee recruitment; and other HEIs use rankings to help identify potential partners, to assess membership of international networks and organizations, and for benchmarking purposes.

student debt. Many governments, most notably Australia and the United Kingdom, have put institutional data online for easy accessibility and comparison. Most radical is the influence of social media: "rate my professor" sites (see, e.g., Students Review, http://www.studentsreview.com/) may be scorned, but they represent a fundamental transformation in assessment of quality beyond the control of the academy, governments, and ranking organizations.

In conclusion, according to the International Association of Universities (2014), there are over 16,000 higher education institutions worldwide, but global rankings focus on the characteristics and performance of the top 100 universities, less than 1%. Obsession with obtaining a place within this group obscures consideration of the wider implications. Two issues stand out. First, measuring higher education performance and quality across diverse contexts is inherently complicated and difficult. Which university is "best" depends upon what question is being asked, who is asking the question, and the purpose of the question. Context is vital. Nonetheless, governments and HEIs seem content to set national and institutional priorities and targets based upon imperfect indicators. Are governments and university leaders abdicating national sovereignty or institutional responsibility to nonrepresentative and commercial interests? If the indicators change, will the strategic goals change? Second, global rankings use indicators that predominantly measure research or research-related activity; this equates to 100% in ARWU, 85% in THE, and 70% in QS. These data are the easiest to find, but they destabilize higher education's wider mission and encourage prestige-seeking by being more selective. As HEIs pursue world-class status, are they being transformed into private, self-serving entities concerned with their individual global position and less engaged or committed to their nations or regions?

These developments represent a significant challenge to democratic societies. Higher education is vital to fuel and sustain personal, social, and economic development; its status and reputation are now also a critical component of a wider geopolitical struggle. Many of the reforms currently being pursued are both necessary and inevitable—and arguably late in coming. With the onslaught of global rankings, higher education has come under the spotlight in a very intense way. The stakes are high for both nations and HEIs. It will be difficult to put the genie back into the bottle.

References

Altbach, P., & Salmi, J. (Eds.). (2011). *The road to academic excellence: The making of world-class research universities*. Washington, DC: World Bank.
Anderson, N., & Rucker, P. (2013, August 22). Obama proposes college-rating system that could increase affordability. *Washington Post*. Retrieved from http://www.washingtonpost.com/politics/obama-to-propose-college-ranking-system-that-could-increase-affordability/2013/08/22/73e674c0-0b17-11e3-b87c-476db8ac34cd_story.html

Becker, G. S. (1993). Nobel lecture: The economic way of looking at behavior. *Journal of Political Economy, 101*(3), 385–409.

Billal, F. (n.d.). *Academic ranking of universities: Healthy competition, setting hierarchy or intelligent marketing?* Paris, France: United Nations Educational, Scientific and Cultural Organization. Retrieved from http://www.unesco.org/new/fileadmin/MULTIMEDIA/HQ/ED/pdf/RANKINGS/Ranking%20of%20universities_%20Paris 2011.pdf

Bourdieu, P. (1986). The forms of capital. In J. Richardson (Ed.), *Handbook of theory and research for the sociology of education* (pp. 241–258). New York, NY: Greenwood Press.

Carpenter, T. (2011, August 17). Brownback seeks higher academic rankings. *The Topeka Capital-Journal.* Retrieved from http://cjonline.com/news/2011-08-17/ brownback-seeks-higher-academic-rankings

Castells, M. (1996). *The rise of the network society: The information age: Economy, society and culture.* Malden, MA: Blackwell.

Clarke, M. (2007). The impact of higher education rankings on student access, choice, and opportunity. In J. P. Merisotis, A. F. Cunningham, A. M. Kee, T. Gordon, & L. H. Leegwater (Eds.), *College and university ranking systems: Global perspectives, American challenges* (pp. 35–49). Washington, DC: Institute of Higher Education Policy.

Dichev, I. (2001). News or noise? Estimating the noise in the U.S. News university rankings. *Research in Higher Education, 42*(3), 237–266.

Ederer, P., Schuler, P., & Wills, S. (2008). *University systems ranking: Citizens and society in the age of knowledge.* Brussels, Belgium: The Lisbon Council.

Ferlie, E., Musselin, C., & Andresani, G. (2008). The steering of higher education systems: A public management perspective. *Higher Education, 56*(3), 325–348.

Flick, C. M., & Convoco Foundation. (2011). *Geographies of the world's knowledge.* Oxford, UK: Oxford Internet Institute, University of Oxford.

Foucault, M. (1977). *Discipline and punish. The birth of the prison.* London, UK: Penguin Books.

Frank, R. H. (2001). Higher education: The ultimate winner-take-all market? In M. Devlin & J. Meyerson (Eds.), *Forum futures: Exploring the future of higher education* (pp. 3–12) [2000 Papers, Forum Strategy Series, 3]. San Francisco, CA: Jossey-Bass.

Goswami, U. A. (2014, January 6). Times higher education to add India-specific parameters to ranking. *The Economic Times.* Retrieved from http://articles.economictimes .indiatimes.com/2014-01-06/news/45918772_1_world-university-rankings-foreign -students-times-higher-education

Gramsci, A. (1971). Critical notes on an attempt at popular sociology. In Q. Hoare & G. N. Smith (Eds & Trans.), *Selections from the prison notebooks of Antonio Gramsci* (pp. 419–472). London, UK: Lawrence and Wishart.

Hazelkorn, E. (2007). The impact of league tables and rankings systems on higher education decision-making. *Higher Education Management and Policy, 19*(2), 87–110.

Hazelkorn, E. (2009). *The impact of global rankings on higher education research and the production of knowledge* [UNESCO Forum on Higher Education, Research and Knowledge Occasional Paper No. 16]. Paris, France: United Nations Educational, Scientific and Cultural Organization.

Hazelkorn, E. (2011). *Rankings and the reshaping of higher education: The battle for world class excellence.* Basingstoke, UK: Palgrave Macmillan.

Hazelkorn, E. (2013, September/October). Europe enters the college ranking game. *Washington Monthly.* Retrieved from http://www.washingtonmonthly.com/magazine /september_october_2013/features/europe_enters_the_college_rank046894.php? page=all

Hazelkorn, E. (2014a). Striving for "world class excellence": Rankings and emerging societies. In D. Araya & P. Marber (Eds.), *Higher education in the global age: Policy, practice and promise in emerging societies* (pp. 246–270). New York, NY: Routledge.

Hazelkorn, E. (2014b). The effect of rankings on student choice and institutional selection. In B. W. A. Jongbloed & J. J. Vossensteyn (Eds.), *Access and expansion post-massification: Opportunities and barriers to further growth in higher education participation.* London, UK: Routledge.

Higher Education Research Institute. (2007). *College rankings & college choice.* Los Angeles: University of California. Retrieved from http://www.heri.ucla.edu/PDFs /pubs/briefs/brief-081707-CollegeRankings.pdf

Hirsch, F. (1997). *The social limits to growth.* London, UK: Routledge.

Hoover, E. (2010, November 5). Application inflation. *The Chronicle of Higher Education.* Retrieved from http://chronicle.com/article/Application-Inflation/125277/

International Association of Universities. (2014). *International handbook of universities.* Basingstoke, UK: Palgrave Macmillan.

Jöns, H., & Hoyler, M. (2013). Global geographies of higher education: The perspective of world university rankings. *Geoforum, 46,* 45–59.

Kishkovsky, S. (2012, March 5). Russia moves to improve its university ranking. *The New York Times.* Retrieved from http://www.nytimes.com/2012/03/26/world/europe /russia-moves-to-improve-its-university-rankings.html?pagewanted=all&_r=1&

Lederman, D. (2005, December 6). Angling for the top 20. *Inside Higher Ed.* Retrieved from http://www.insidehighered.com/news/2005/12/06/kentucky

Lo, W. Y. W. (2011). Soft power, university rankings and knowledge production: Distinctions between hegemony and self-determination in higher education. *Comparative Education, 47*(2), 209–222.

Marginson, S. (2009). University rankings, government and social order: Managing the field of higher education according to the logic of the performative present-as-future. In M. Simons, M. Olssen, & M. Peters (Eds.), *Re-reading education policies: Studying the policy agenda of the 21st century* (pp. 584–604). Rotterdam, the Netherlands: Sense.

Marginson, S., & van der Wende, M. (2007). *Globalisation and higher education* [OECD Education Working Paper No. 8]. Paris, France: Organisation for Economic Co-operation and Development.

Nanda, P. K. (2013, May 22). India to lobby foreign agencies for improving university rankings. *Live Mint & The Wall Street Journal.* Retrieved from http:// www.livemint.com/Politics/X1xJY3phY6DwwFkWyG3sPO/India-to-lobby-foreign -agencies-for-improving-university-ran.html

Organisation for Economic Co-operation and Development (OECD). (2013). *Education at a glance 2013. OECD indicators.* Paris, France: Author.

Pryor, J. H., Eagan, K., Blake, L. P., Hurtado, S., Berdan, J., & Case, M. H. (2012). *The American freshman: National norms fall 2012.* Los Angeles: Higher Education Research Institute, University of California.

Raju, P. (2014, January 18). IITs to compete as single unit in world university rankings. Retrieved from http://www.indiaeducationreview.com/news/iits-compete-single -unit-world-university-rankings/14997

Reback, R., & Alter, M. (2014). True for your school? How changing reputations alter demand for selective U.S. colleges. *Educational Evaluation and Policy Analysis, 36*(1), 1–25.

Reich, R. B. (2000, September 15). How selective colleges heighten inequality. *The Chronicle of Higher Education.* Retrieved from http://chronicle.com/article /How-Selective-Colleges/26250

Salmi, J. (2009). *The challenge of establishing world class universities: Directions in human development.* Washington, DC: World Bank.

Santiago, P., Tremblay, K., Basri, E., & Arnal, E. (2008). *Tertiary education for the knowledge society* (Vol. 1). Paris, France: Organisation for Economic Co-operation and Development.

Sauder, M., & Espeland, W. N. (2009). The discipline of rankings: Tight coupling and organizational change. *American Sociological Review, 74*(1), 63–82.

Sauder, M., & Lancaster, R. (2006). Do rankings matter? The effects of U.S. News and World Report rankings on the admissions process of law schools. *Law and Society Review, 40*(1), 105–134.

Schmalbeck, R. (1998). The durability of law school reputation. *Journal of Legal Education, 48*(4), 568–590.

Slaughter, S., & Leslie, L. (1997). *Academic capitalism: Politics, policies and the entrepreneurial university.* Baltimore, MD: Johns Hopkins University Press.

Smith, K. (2002). *What is the "knowledge economy"? Knowledge intensity and distributed knowledge bases* [United Nations Discussion Paper]. Maastricht, the Netherlands. Retrieved from http://eprints.utas.edu.au/1235/

Sponsler, B. A. (2009). *The role and relevance of rankings in higher education policymaking.* Washington, DC: Institute of Higher Education Policy.

Tight, M. (2000). Do league tables contribute to the development of a quality culture? *Higher Education Quarterly, 54*(1), 22–42.

Walker, T. (2004, November 12). Educating the elite. *DW-World.* Retrieved from http://www.dw.de/educating-the-elite/a-1393321-1

Washington Monthly. (2013). *College guide.* Retrieved from http://www.washingtonmonthly.com/college_guide/toc_2013.php

Webster, D. S. A. (1986). *Academic quality rankings of American colleges and universities.* Springfield, IL: Charles C. Thomas.

Williams, R., de Rassenfosse, G., Jensen, P., & Marginson, S. (2012/2013). *U21 rankings of national higher education systems.* Melbourne, Australia: University of Melbourne.

Winston, G. C. (2000). *The positional arms race in higher education* [Discussion Paper No. 54, Williams Project on the Economics of Higher Education]. Williamstown, MA: Williams College.

ELLEN HAZELKORN *holds a joint appointment as director, Higher Education Policy Research Unit, Dublin Institute of Technology, and policy advisor, Higher Education Authority, Ireland.*

3

This chapter provides a critical perspective on the global quest to build world-class universities (WCUs), including global "ranking mania," excessive emphasis on university branding, and the attending threats to the traditional public good mission of the university. Alternatively, we offer suggestions on how rankings may be used to advance a social justice vision of WCUs.

The Global Quest to Build World-Class Universities: Toward a Social Justice Agenda

Robert A. Rhoads, Shuai Li, Lauren Ilano

The rapid nature of change in the global higher education arena over the past two decades has roused an upsurge of discourse about the new academic arms race: the quest to build world-class universities (WCUs). As the new knowledge-based economy gains ascendency in the context of postindustrial and information-based societies, the importance of high-level research universities has been heightened (Altbach & Balán, 2007; Rhoads, Wang, Shi, & Chang, 2014; Slaughter & Rhoades, 2004). Research universities are touted as centers for knowledge production and "flagships for postsecondary education worldwide" (Altbach, 2011, p. 11). The emerging archetypical model of the global research university, based on the threefold mission of teaching, research, and service, is to a great extent based on the U.S. model (Mohrman, Ma, & Baker, 2008; Rhoads, 2011). Despite the multifaceted roles flagship universities play, it is the research mission that has come to dominate a growing hierarchy of universities (Altbach, 2011). As Ellen Hazelkorn explains in Chapter 2 of this volume, the hegemony of the research-dominant model of the university has been reinforced by global ranking schemes that confer world-class status upon select institutions. Thus, global rankings have become a key element of the emerging discourse on WCUs and are influencing institutional aspirations as well as national policies.

The global quest to develop WCUs is extensive and has spread across both developed and developing nations. For developing and rising nations, attaining WCU status is a marker of national economic competitiveness;

NEW DIRECTIONS FOR HIGHER EDUCATION, no. 168, Winter 2014 © 2014 Wiley Periodicals, Inc.
Published online in Wiley Online Library (wileyonlinelibrary.com) • DOI: 10.1002/he.20111

27

thus, government support of top research universities may be considered an investment in a nation's future. For example, Byun, Jon, and Kim (2013) pointed to the role the South Korean government has played in advancing programs to cultivate its WCUs through capital investment in projects to strengthen research productivity and quality. Vorotnikov (2013) identified a similar trend in Russia, where the government allocated the equivalent of $20 million to top research universities to assist in their quest to achieve world-class standing by 2020. China has also pursued the development of WCUs, allocating billions of Chinese *yuan* to a group of more than 100 leading universities (Rhoads et al., 2014). Ngok and Guo (2008) identified the converging interests of the Chinese government and the nation's top universities in creating WCUs to increase China's economic standing in the growing knowledge economy.

The desire to be considered world-class is not confined to developing or rising nations seeking to establish themselves globally. For instance, a main aspect of the "Lisbon Strategy," developed by the European Council in 2000, was elevation of the European economy by placing great emphasis on strengthening higher education (Deem, Mok, & Lucas, 2008). The relationship between the national economy and university development is also evident in Australia's attempt to build a world-class system as opposed to individual WCUs. As Sheil (2010) demonstrated, Australia's desire to maintain a world-class system stems from the economic incentive of exporting educational services. State-sponsored assistance in Australia, therefore, spans the entire higher education sector without any "explicit strategy of developing elite, flagship institutions to serve as a beacon for the entire system" (Sheil, 2010, p. 75).

The aforementioned examples of world-class aspirations serve to demonstrate the expansiveness of competitive changes occurring across the globe. The reality of increasing competition for world-class status among research universities (and their home nations) has raised numerous problems. First, the competition among universities, based to a great extent on their position relative to the new knowledge economy, is fueled by institutional rankings that largely serve to reinforce preexisting hierarchies (Marginson, 2007; Marginson & van der Wende, 2007; Rhoads, 2011). Although wealthy, elite universities have the financial flexibility to adapt to the prevailing ranking schemes, less wealthy universities typically do not. Additionally, the dominance of leading universities in a handful of wealthy nations calls us to question the normative quality of the global rankings that classify WCUs and the degree to which this trend is beneficial for the world's higher education systems. As rankings create elitist hierarchies, clearly attended to by the leading nations of the world, the fear of global homogenization and hegemony becomes a reality (Rhoads, 2011). The quest for global recognition and reputation thus threatens more localized considerations universities ought to address as part of their contribution to the public good. By "public good," we largely refer to social responsibilities universities inherit as part of their obligation to the societies in which they operate; we are not suggesting that universities are not also responsible for global concerns, but rather that such forms of engagement should not come at the expense of local matters (Rhoads & Szelényi, 2011).

In this chapter, we propose án alternative to the research-driven, wealth-based emphasis of the current quest to develop WCUs. As they stand, global rankings serve to limit the vision of institutions by incentivizing homogenous global ambition over localized contributions. We propose various ways to alter rankings in order to redirect the competition toward a more socially just orientation, focusing on the ways universities may be judged based on their contributions and service to local communities and disadvantaged populations. Although the global terrain of higher education will inevitably be changed by the high tech, information-based knowledge economy, the more localized, public good function of the university should not be lost in the fray. Because we see no signs of global rankings being eliminated any time soon, we have decided to join the dialogue by suggesting ways of altering ranking schemes so as to advance a social justice vision of WCUs.

The Meaning and Rationale of World-Class Universities

Many universities throughout the world pursue WCU status. Altbach (2009) noted that obtaining world-class status involves the capacity of universities to produce quality research, whereas Salmi (2009) posited that "world-class" signifies not only the effort to improve teaching or research in higher education but also "the capacity to compete in the global tertiary education marketplace through the acquisition, adaptation, and creation of advanced knowledge" (p. 4). He further argued that status as world-class is not a matter of self-proclamation, but instead is conferred through global acknowledgement. Before the 2003 emergence of Shanghai Jiaotong University's *Academic Ranking of World Universities (ARWU)*, which adopted systematic methodologies in an attempt to objectively measure worldwide universities' academic capacity, "global acknowledgement" only involved reputation, a relatively subjective measure lacking in rigor.

One explanation for the rise of ranking schemes such as *ARWU*, *Times Higher Education (THE) World University Rankings*, and the *Quacquarelli Sydmonds (QS) World University Rankings* is the reality that higher education has become a global commodity that is still growing exponentially (Gürüz, 2011). The growing demand for postsecondary education, the increasing availability and accessibility of learning materials, advanced modes of transportation, and improved educational technologies all interact to facilitate the formulation of a complex global marketplace (Gürüz, 2011). New forms of transportation and technology break down the boundaries of time and geography, and as a result, today's higher education institutions (HEIs) function as more than disseminators of common knowledge and local values—they also aim to serve a more expansive international community. The changing notion of community alters the behaviors of HEIs and accelerates global competition for resources (Daniel, Leavitt, & Romer, 1998). Many nations pour enormous funds into their leading universities, with ambition to create WCUs. Great pressure is placed on universities to compete for the most talented and/or revenue-generating students, for merit-based research funding and grants, for highly influential faculties, and for highly skilled staff (Marginson, 2006).

Another factor that helps to explain the press to establish WCUs is the emergence of the knowledge-based economy. The Organisation for Economic Co-operation and Development (OECD, 1999) defined a nation with a knowledge-based economy as one where "the production, diffusion and use of technology and information are key to economic activity and sustainable growth" (p. 7). Salmi (2009) summarized four strategic dimensions to an analytical framework, initially proposed by the World Bank, to facilitate nations' transition to a knowledge-based economy: a suitable regime for economy and institution, a strong human capital base that expedites absorption and utilization of knowledge, a solid and active information infrastructure, and a supportive national innovation system. Universities uniquely integrate and generate synergy among all four dimensions, with their most fundamental roles arguably being the development of human capital and the production of new knowledge and technologies to be transformed into economic growth (Salmi, 2009). Thus, in the context of an increasingly interconnected world economy, ambitious developing or rising nations seek rapid growth and active participation in the international economy, whereas more developed nations look to maintain their dominance. Regardless of status as "developing" or "developed," or something in between, the reality is that universities play a key role in economic development.

Various renditions of the WCU idea have been discussed in terms of an increasingly globalized economy, including the Emerging Global Model or EGM (Mohrman et al., 2008). EGMs compete for students, faculty, and funding with their peers worldwide, in a context in which traditional political limitations, linguistic barriers, and access boundaries are diminished. The EGM is an intensified and globalized version of the research university, emphasizing a global vision and advanced research capacity. Though fully developed EGMs are still limited, they can be distinguished from a broader range of HEIs based on several key characteristics, including a global mission, international collaboration, worldwide recruitment, and intensified emphasis on research.

What becomes fairly obvious in reviewing relevant literature is that the meaning of world-class tends to point in the same direction: to one ideal model of the university—the comprehensive, research-intensive university. Here again, rankings play a key role in limiting the essential characteristics of WCUs (Marginson & van der Wende, 2007). For example, Marginson (2007) noted that any system of university rankings is driven by purpose, with specific assumptions preset and particular values weighted over others. Thus, all ranking systems are biased and incomplete in terms of capturing the complex dynamics of potential WCUs. In defense of research productivity factors dominating the global schemes, Marginson and van der Wende (2007) argued that the comprehensive research-intensive university is the only type of HEI that exists globally, and hence is the only type that can be compared at a worldwide level. Yet, even research-intensive universities have obligations extending beyond simply accumulating research funding and research-related outcomes.

The Quest for World-Class Status and Global "Ranking Mania"

As noted in Ellen Hazelkorn's chapter, the global reputation race is—for better or for worse—central to how we understand higher education competition and the significance of the pursuit of world-class standing. Global ranking, or what we see as global "ranking mania," has come to dominate the discussion of WCUs. As noted, global ranking criteria for the top ranking schemes (*ARWU*, *THE*, and *QS*) tend to focus on research and research-related outcome measures. For example, the *ARWU* rankings include measures such as the following: alumni and staff winning Fields Medals and Nobel Prizes, measures of highly cited researchers, number of articles published in *Nature* and *Science*, and number of articles indexed in the Science Citation Index Expanded (SCI Expanded) and the Social Sciences Citation Index (SSCI; ARWU, 2013). *THE World University Rankings* groups 13 performance indicators into five domains, with "research" and "citations" accounting for a combined 60% of the overall performance score (THE, 2013). Similarly, the *QS World University Rankings* (QS, 2013) stress "academic peer review" (40%), which is essentially a measure of institutional status, but also relies on citation counts per faculty member (20%).

The research emphasis of global ranking methodologies leads to several problems, with the most obvious consequence being elevation of one type of WCU—the research university. The heavy emphasis nations in turn place on research universities potentially leads to other types of colleges and universities being neglected, which works against the advancement of a diversified higher education system and variable understandings of WCUs. A problem here is that universities in diverse nations need to develop with an eye to specific economic and cultural conditions; they should be inspired to serve multiple purposes and work to implement particular strategies suitable to the needs of the populations and communities in which they reside. We are not rejecting globalization, but merely suggesting that global ranking schemes disproportionately alter the balance between local and global concerns.

Global ranking mania has captivated many leaders and policy makers involved in higher education, especially in terms of particular HEIs seeking increased institutional prestige (Rhoads et al., 2014); the latter tendency leads to widespread forms of mission drift and institutional isomorphism (DiMaggio & Powell, 1983). Given the present ranking systems, the primary way to improve an institution's standing is to emphasize the heaviest weighted performance indicators, which leads a university to imitate the institutional structure of the highest ranked universities. In this manner, one might argue that university governance, strategic planning, organizational characteristics, and curricular arrangements are converging toward those commonly recognized as part of WCUs (Vaira, 2004).

Additional consequences, based on pressures to generate greater streams of research revenue (given outcome measures tied to research capacity), may involve universities drifting away from their social responsibility to serve the public good. The relationship between research revenue and WCU status promotes institutional behaviors that, for instance, are not necessarily oriented toward serving students, improving teaching quality, or attending to diverse student needs, given that addressing such concerns exerts little to no influence on a university's ranking. Moreover, the needs of students from low-income backgrounds might be entirely ignored because this concern has no direct connection to the vast majority of ranking schemes. But with ranking schemes tied so directly to the accumulation of funds and institutional wealth—which serve as an overall predictor of a university's rank—it should come as no surprise that marketizing and commercializing universities and their products have taken on aggressive new forms. Nowhere is this more obvious than in the arena of university branding.

Excesses of University Branding

As international rankings add fuel to the race for WCU status, universities have turned to branding as a tool for establishing a market niche. Given the growing global marketplace for higher education, building the capacity of universities to compete as global brands is viewed as increasingly important. Branding refers to concerted marketing efforts that effactually bond an external image or logo to an organizational identity (Stensaker, 2007). As university competition for world-class status becomes the norm in global higher education, universities seek to brand themselves in new ways by using forms of rhetoric, symbolism, and commercialization that increasingly tie them to the marketplace. We see two major forms of branding and marketization as significant to expanding global visibility: (a) the rise of online courses, particularly massive open online courses (MOOCs); and (b) university merchandising efforts.

The digital frontier, embodied by Internet-based instructional technology and open educational resources (OER), has been pursued by speculative institutions since early 2000 but has grown exponentially since 2004 (OECD, 2007). MOOCs, representing a recent rendition of this speculative Internet-based environment, essentially provide virtual courses free of charge (Rhoads, Berdan, & Toven-Lindsey, 2013). Despite their high costs of implementation and a lack of tangible income, the concept of MOOCs, as well as the actual courses, has expanded globally. Certainly, the opportunity to provide free course materials around the world has been stressed as a positive in terms of democratizing knowledge, and world-class universities such as Massachusetts Institute of Technology (MIT) and Harvard have taken the lead on this initiative. But there is another facet to the promotion of one's own course materials at a global level—something likely achievable only by the most elite universities—and that is the possibility to dominate the global marketplace through Internet-based branding. The possibility of offering MIT or Harvard courses to anyone around the world is contingent to a great extent on the status potential learners associate with these institutions, while at the same time such possibilities generate incredible name recognition, arguably furthering the universities' brands and elevating their status. The potential of MOOCs internationally gives elite institutions a vehicle by which to provide a sampling of course offerings and expand the scope of institutional branding. In essence, anyone can have a piece of the Harvard or MIT experience, although the "piece" they experience has little resemblance to the brick-and-mortar version. The strategy of building branch campuses abroad, as New York University has done in various locales around the world, may serve similar global branding goals.

A second type of branding involves a more direct form of merchandising. For example, the University of California, Los Angeles (UCLA) created an international clothing line—a UCLA brand—with items that can be purchased through the Internet or at a local mall in China. One can stroll through the fashionable Zhongguancun Mall in Beijing, wander into a third-floor clothing store known simply as "UCLA," and leave adorned with any number of shirts, hats, and jackets incorporating the UCLA logo. This type of commercialization and branding of the university raises serious questions about the role of increased marketization in higher education. The product itself—for example, a shirt with a university name or logo—has no direct tie to the traditional functions of the university, though arguably such marketization does attempt to capitalize on the values of the university. As a case in point, the UCLA brand boasts in its advertising: "With a top academic record, an unrivalled sporting legacy and the beautiful California backdrop, UCLA has a long-standing global following" (UCLA Clothing, 2013, para. 1). UCLA is attempting to establish a marketable product for revenue generation, while simultaneously marketing the global renown of its institutional achievements. This form of university branding extends far beyond what might normally be associated with a university in terms of the commodification of research and teaching products.

The hypercommercialization of the university as a brand, promoted as part of expanding international reputation, leads one to question what such a trend signifies within the context of global competitiveness and status as a WCU. A belief in universities as social institutions that are accountable to serving the public good—such as providing access for low-income populations—seems threatened as universities increasingly adopt and adapt to a multitude of practices redefining the nature and scope of their own identities. In other words, they appear less like nonprofit entities engaged in service to society, and instead increasingly resemble global corporate enterprises. Furthermore, as global, market-based competition increases among universities—fueled to a great extent by global ranking mania—superficial market practices may become the "new normal." With the preceding in mind, and given the potential for globalized commercialization and branding to dominate the idea of WCUs, we see the need to propose alternatives to the present global ranking schemes.

Advancing a Social Justice Vision

As marketization—evidenced in part by excessive branding practices—becomes more common among universities competing for WCU status, the organizational identity and core values of the university appear to be changing. But aggressive branding practices are only representative of surface-level changes occurring within universities. Far deeper changes are taking place at the level of value orientation. At the heart of the problem is the norming function of rankings and the quest for WCU standing, as evidenced by the homogeneity of output measures. As they presently stand, the criteria most prevalent in rankings are similar across the board: research productivity, student selectivity, and publications and awards. Part of our concern is that these measures tend to be proxies for institutional wealth (Pusser & Marginson, 2013). Therefore, institutions that are able to amass funding and hire prolific researchers tend to fare more favorably (which also serves to further their institutional status). The corresponding pressures to emphasize research output can lead universities to direct their attention and aspirations in a manner disconnected from their social responsibilities, especially those of a local variety. As global rankings and the quest for a narrowly defined notion of WCUs further push universities into competition with one another, their mission of public good is compromised. Although many have lamented the threats that marketization and commercialization pose to higher education as a social institution, as a democratic public sphere, and as a purveyor of the public good (e.g., Giroux, 2002; Gumport, 2000; Rhoads & Rhoades, 2005), few have proposed ways that rankings might in fact advance or support a social justice vision of the university.

Although rankings tend to be somewhat ignored by scholars critical of the growing market-dominant, WCU-driven model and ideals of the university, the impetus for global rankings and university hierarchization will likely not disappear anytime soon. This means that without alternative points of view—especially those consistent with a social justice orientation—the hegemony of the present rankings will only be strengthened. In what ways might we derail the current renditions in favor of models more supportive of a public good vision of the university?

One concern we have about the current dominant ranking schemes is the external focus institutions seeking to attain WCU standing demand. Rather than focusing so strongly on general research output and associated monies accumulated to fund research activity, we recommend incorporating university contributions to local communities into the rankings. For example, the percentage of institutional revenues dedicated to community outreach or public service may be used as a marker for institutional commitment to local needs. This could take many forms, including supporting university-based efforts to strengthen mentorship and tutoring programs in low-income and underresourced K–12 schools or offering educational assistance to underrepresented minority populations. It could be as simple as this: What percentage of institutional spending is devoted to such activities? Certainly, various categories and distinctions would need to be worked out, given national and cultural differences, but this is also true of current ranking systems.

We also propose taking into account student, staff, and faculty dedication to public service and public good enterprises, such as supporting public schools or nonprofit organizations. Regarding students and public service measures, we recommend two possibilities or derivations. First, a measure could be developed that examines the percentage of students involved in community or public service. A second measure could focus on the extent of such student engagement, in terms of average hours per week or per term. Similar measures could be developed with regard to faculty and staff; again, both percentage of participation and extensiveness of service to public good enterprises could be assessed.

Possible inroads also exist in terms of how research is measured and the degree to which social justice measures may be incorporated into such metrics. Currently, research measures tend to stress the extensiveness of research funding and research outcomes (e.g., articles in indexed journals) as well as highly specific measures such as number of faculty winning the most prestigious research awards (e.g., the Fields Medal). These tend to favor the wealthiest and most elite universities, but what if universities were evaluated on the basis of allocating research funds to public good enterprises, such as public health? For example, medical research is highly valued by research universities under the current global ranking system due in part to the substantial amount of research output and enormous funding involved; thus, funding in this area can significantly impact a university's positioning in the rankings. But how can such measures be redesigned to emphasize less revenue-focused medical research, such as that which largely addresses public health issues?

In addition to medical research, there are other research-related activities that might be refashioned with social justice concerns in mind. What if measures were implemented to examine a university's research support for nonprofit or community-based organizations? Returning to the previous example concerning mentorship and tutoring programs in low-income and underresourced schools, what percentage of an institution's research spending targets such endeavors? One could also measure the percentage of soft or hard research monies aimed at addressing community needs through existing university channels and/or mechanisms. Also, to what degree is a university committed to participatory action research programs as a means to contribute to improving living conditions for economically disadvantaged populations?

Another concern, one relating directly to the social justice vision of a university, is the fact that the social mobility contribution of universities is entirely ignored by the current global ranking systems that lead to WCU status. Again, metrics the three most popular global ranking schemes utilize are largely related to a university's ability to carry out extensive research. The heavy emphasis on research and research-related outcomes fails to capture other important contributions WCUs can make, such as expanding diversity and addressing forms of inequality. Ranking schemes need to increasingly adopt a public good perspective, especially regarding some of the important social responsibilities WCUs have to their respective societies.

Although it may not be realistic to demand that global ranking systems incorporate all social equity concerns at once, it does seem feasible to begin by integrating some basic social mobility measures. For example, rankings could consider measures related to the percentage of students from the bottom third or fourth of family income distribution within a respective nation who graduate within five to six years. A similar idea specific to the U.S. context comes from *The Washington Monthly*, which uses a measure involving the graduation rates of Pell Grant recipients, given that qualifying for a Pell Grant essentially defines a student as economically challenged. In China, a similar idea might involve examining the graduation rates of students qualifying for the National Student Loan program, an indicator of being economically disadvantaged in that country. Similar kinds of measures could potentially examine the participation and graduation rates of underrepresented racial or ethnic populations. We also suggest that a range of marginalized populations be considered in promoting measures of inclusiveness, including lesbian, gay, bisexual, and transgendered people. In terms of women in STEM-related fields traditionally dominated by men, universities could be assessed on the basis of the participation and graduation rates of female students.

With regard to faculty and staff, measures of institutional inclusiveness could be developed on the basis of meaningful representation of underrepresented ethnic or racial minorities as well as women. For example, what is the percentage of women at various faculty ranks at a particular university and how does it compare to other universities? In their study of the experiences of female academics in China, Rhoads and Gu (2012) highlighted the ongoing challenges women face, especially in terms of failing to progress to the most senior levels of the professorate. With regard to rankings and opportunities for women, Rhoads and Gu (2012) raised this important question: "What impact might such rankings have on the betterment of opportunities for academic women, at a global level, if they actually required universities to report gender data and then used such data in their complex ranking schemas?" (p. 747). Implementing such measures does not seem overwhelmingly difficult, although one might reasonably question the institutional commitment to advancing such an idea. Perhaps pressure from powerful nongovernmental organizations and transnational women's organizations could help to push such an idea forward.

Conclusion

As the result of global ranking mania, a more homogenized and global version of what it means to achieve WCU standing is gaining strength. Another consequence of the global push to build WCUs is the way today's universities have compromised their mission to serve the public good by adopting behaviors heavily influenced by a marketized and commercialized ideal. Excessive university branding reflects another form of quest for world-class standing, as universities increasingly embrace corporatized practices.

Considering the dominance of marketization and commercialization, as well as the role of rankings in defining the key features of WCUs, we propose a university ranking scheme based on measures of social justice. We put forward several suggestions, including incorporating the following: university contributions to local communities; contributions to nonprofit and public good organizations (e.g., public schools); metrics regarding research outputs linked to public good issues, such as public health; and measures that assess a university's commitment to promoting inclusiveness. Future research might consider looking into the potential of social justice schemes and the ways in which the various cultural complexities of globalized measures might be incorporated as part of the quest to build WCUs.

References

Academic Ranking of World Universities (ARWU). (2013). *Academic Ranking of World Universities methodology*. Retrieved from http://www.shanghairanking.com /ARWU-Methodology-2013.html

Altbach, P. G. (2009). Peripheries and centers: Research universities in developing countries. *Asia Pacific Education Review, 10*(1), 15–27.

Altbach, P. G. (2011). The past, present, and future of the research university. In P. G. Altbach & J. Salmi (Eds.), *The road to academic excellence: The making of world-class research universities* (pp. 11–32). Washington, DC: The World Bank.

Altbach, P. G., & Balán, J. (2007). *World class worldwide: Transforming research universities in Asia and Latin America*. Baltimore, MD: Johns Hopkins University Press.

Byun, K., Jon, J.-E., & Kim, D. (2013). Quest for building world-class universities in South Korea: Outcomes and consequences. *Higher Education, 65*, 645–659.

Daniel, J., Leavitt, M., & Romer, R. (1998). Perspectives on higher education in the global market. *Cause/Effect, 21*(3), 11–18.

Deem, R., Mok, K. H., & Lucas, L. (2008). Transforming higher education in whose image? Exploring the concept of the "world-class" university in Europe and Asia. *Higher Education Policy, 21*, 83–97.

DiMaggio, P. J., & Powell, W. W. (1983). The iron cage revisited: Institutional isomorphism and collective rationality in organization fields. *American Sociological Review, 48*(2), 147–160.

Giroux, H. A. (2002). Neoliberalism, corporate culture, and the promise of higher education: The university as a democratic public sphere. *Harvard Educational Review, 72*(4), 425–464.

Gumport, P. J. (2000). Academic restructuring: Organizational change and institutional imperatives. *Higher Education, 39*(1), 67–91.

Gürüz, K. (2011). *Higher education and international student mobility in the global knowledge economy.* Albany, NY: SUNY Press.

Marginson, S. (2006). Dynamics of national and global competition in higher education. *Higher Education, 52*(1), 1–39.

Marginson, S. (2007). *Global university rankings: Where to from here?* Melbourne, Australia: Centre for the Study of Higher Education, University of Melbourne.

Marginson, S., & van der Wende, M. (2007). To rank or to be ranked: The impact of global rankings in higher education. *Journal of Studies in International Education, 11*(3–4), 306–329.

Mohrman, K., Ma, W., & Baker, D. (2008). The research university in transition: The emerging global model. *Higher Education Policy, 21*(1), 5–27.

Ngok, K., & Guo, W. (2008). The quest for world class universities in China: Critical reflections. *Policy Futures in Education, 6*(5), 545–557.

Organisation for Economic Co-operation and Development (OECD). (1999). *The knowledge-based economy: A set of facts and figures.* Paris, France: Author.

Organisation for Economic Co-operation and Development (OECD). (2007). *Giving knowledge for free: The emergence of open educational resources.* Paris, France: Author.

Pusser, B., & Marginson, S. (2013). University rankings in critical perspective. *The Journal of Higher Education, 84*(4), 544–568.

Quacquarelli Sydmonds (QS). (2013). *Ranking methodology.* Retrieved from http://www.topuniversities.com/university-rankings-articles/world-university-rankings/qs-world-university-rankings-methodology

Rhoads, R. A. (2011). The U.S. research university as a global model: Some fundamental problems to consider. *InterActions, 7*(2), Article 4 [Online journal]. Retrieved from http://escholarship.org/uc/item/8b91s24r

Rhoads, R. A., Berdan, J., & Toven-Lindsey, B. (2013). The open courseware movement in higher education: Unmasking power and raising questions about the movement's democratic potential. *Educational Theory, 63*(1), 87–109.

Rhoads, R. A., & Gu, D. Y. (2012). A gendered point of view on the challenges of women academics in The People's Republic of China. *Higher Education, 63*(6), 733–750.

Rhoads, R. A., & Rhoades, G. (2005). Graduate employee unionization as symbol of and challenge to the corporatization of U.S. research universities. *Journal of Higher Education, 76*(3), 243–275.

Rhoads, R. A., & Szelényi, K. (2011). *Global citizenship and the university: Advancing social life and relations in an interdependent world.* Stanford, CA: Stanford University Press.

Rhoads, R. A., Wang, X., Shi, X., & Chang, Y. (2014). *China's rising research universities: A new era of global ambition.* Baltimore, MD: Johns Hopkins University Press.

Salmi, J. (2009). *The challenge of establishing world-class universities.* Washington, DC: The World Bank.

Sheil, T. (2010). Moving beyond university rankings: Developing a world class university system in Australia. *Australian Universities' Review, 52*(1), 69–76.

Slaughter, S., & Rhoades, G. (2004). *Academic capitalism and the new economy: Markets, state and higher education.* Baltimore, MD: Johns Hopkins University Press.

Stensaker, B. (2007). The relationship between branding and organisational change. *Higher Education Management and Policy, 19*(1), 1–17.

Times Higher Education (THE). (2013). *World University Rankings 2013–2014 methodology.* Retrieved from http://www.timeshighereducation.co.uk/world-university-rankings/2013-14/world-ranking/methodology

University of California, Los Angeles (UCLA) Clothing. (2013). *UCLA clothing history.* Retrieved from http://www.uclaclothing.com/history.php

Vaira, M. (2004). Globalization and higher education organizational change: A framework for analysis. *Higher Education, 48*(4), 483–510.

Vorotnikov, E. (2013, September 11). Government approves universities for world-class bid. *University World News.* Retrieved from http://www.universityworldnews.com/article.php?story=20130911144451887

ROBERT A. RHOADS *is a professor of higher education and organizational change at University of California, Los Angeles.*

SHUAI LI *is a second-year doctoral student at University of California, Los Angeles, in the Division of Higher Education and Organizational Change.*

LAUREN ILANO *is a first-year doctoral student at University of California, Los Angeles, in the Division of Higher Education and Organizational Change.*

NEW DIRECTIONS FOR HIGHER EDUCATION • DOI: 10.1002/he

4

University mergers have become a common strategy for increasing global competitiveness. In this chapter, the authors analyze the implementation of mergers in Finnish universities from the perspective of social justice as conceived within Finland and other Nordic countries.

University Mergers in Finland: Mediating Global Competition

Jussi Välimaa, Helena Aittola, Jani Ursin

Reformers of higher education often see mergers of universities as a kind of "magic bullet" that would solve all existing or assumed problems of higher education (Harman & Harman, 2003). Typically, the goal of merger operations is more efficient and effective use of resources. This goal indicates that political motivations can be found behind most higher education mergers (Harman & Meek, 2002). Additionally, international research has shown that the nature and processes of mergers are seldom swift and that the outcomes of mergers are not easy to verify (Kyvik & Stensaker, 2013).

The aims of this chapter are, first, to describe university mergers in an international context and, second, to discuss the challenges of mergers from a Finnish perspective. Finland is an interesting case for analysis because of a high demand for and execution of mergers in this nation over the past decade. We analyze empirical studies on Finnish university mergers specifically, supported by international studies on mergers more generally. We also discuss the issue of social justice in relation to mergers, given their potential influence on access to higher education. The equitable distribution of higher education and equal access to educational opportunities are crucial topics to explore in any society interested in promoting social justice (see Robertson & Dale, 2013).

Various definitions of university mergers exist. In this chapter, we define a merger as a process during which two or more higher education institutions (HEIs), or parts of HEIs, are structurally or functionally combined into one entity (Harman & Harman, 2003).

NEW DIRECTIONS FOR HIGHER EDUCATION, no. 168, Winter 2014 © 2014 Wiley Periodicals, Inc.
Published online in Wiley Online Library (wileyonlinelibrary.com) • DOI: 10.1002/he.20112

International Research on Mergers

Globally, mergers have been seen as a driving force for change, particularly in HEIs in Asia, Australia, and Europe (Drowley, Lewis, & Brooks, 2013; Harman, 2002; Kyvik, 2002; Kyvik & Stensaker, 2013; Mao, Du, & Liu, 2009; Mok, 2005). Governments and HEIs generally hope that mergers will create new alignments in research, education, and innovation to respond to the global competitiveness of university systems (Harman & Harman, 2008). The main ideological perspective behind the increasing trend toward mergers is the discourse of neoliberalism, specifically as expressed through the notion of "New Public Management," which promotes the ideas of effectiveness, efficiency, marketization, and competition (Drowley et al., 2013; Harman & Harman, 2008). Globalization, in turn, imposes vigorous pressures on national higher education systems to become involved in university rankings, as Ellen Hazelkorn explains in Chapter 2 of this volume. In this arena of competition, governments and HEIs expect mergers to boost the positions of universities in a number of league tables, which in turn is presumed to improve competition for international research funding (see Ministry of Science Technology and Innovation [Denmark], 2009) and recruitment of the most gifted international faculty members and students by providing attractive academic environments.

Within national contexts, the reasons for merging HEIs often stem from governmental policies to reform and restructure national higher education systems (Cai, 2007; Harman & Meek, 2002; Kyvik & Stensaker, 2013). According to Harman and Harman (2008), however, there is a shift toward institutionally initiated mergers in many countries due to the increasing competition between HEIs. One of the most common justifications for planning and implementing a merger is that it would reduce the number of HEIs, thereby lowering the financial costs of the higher education system (Lang, 2003; Tight, 2013). However, empirical research indicates that mergers have proven to be very costly and the savings have often been overestimated (Locke, 2007). In addition to actors within national higher education policy, various external stakeholders may expect that mergers enhance knowledge production by better taking into account the needs of industry, business, and regional stakeholders. These notions are, in turn, connected with the discourse of the knowledge economy and the entrepreneurial roles universities are expected to play in today's knowledge societies (Aula & Tienari, 2011; Mok, 2005).

A number of scholars who have focused on higher education mergers attempt to understand them as a social phenomenon or trend. Several scholars have examined institutional mergers within the framework of governance and management from the perspective of organizational theory (e.g., Bleiklie & Kogan, 2007; Cai, 2007; Locke, 2007). These studies provide knowledge about the structural factors contributing to merger processes, including financial issues, leadership, management, and

funding it managed to acquire from private sources, following the funding formula of Aalto University (Välimaa, 2011).

In addition to the three government-initiated mergers, three universities (University of Tampere, Tampere University of Technology, and University of Jyväskylä) started a process of cooperation referred to as the "University Alliance," which aimed for "enhanced cooperation" among the three institutions. However, the Ministry of Education and Culture (MoEC) did not support this process and it was discontinued quietly. This shows that only those mergers that were supported by the government were given enough resources to be implemented. We also see clearly how important the MoEC is as a national actor in Finnish (and Nordic) higher education policymaking.

Structural reforms such as these are typical in Finland where the nation state continues to be the strongest actor in the field of higher education policymaking—a common situation in other Nordic countries as well. Typically, within Finnish higher education policymaking, all reforms, including university mergers, are prepared and planned by national committees nominated by the MoEC. Regarding the university mergers discussed earlier, all committees suggested increased cooperation between universities through merger operations (MoEC [Finland], 2007a, 2007b, 2007c). The next government implemented these suggestions, which initiated the mergers in 2010 (Ursin, Aittola, Henderson, & Välimaa, 2010). Scholars have subsequently conducted a number of studies regarding the structural changes and merging processes in Finnish universities (see, e.g., Aarrevaara, Dobson, & Elander, 2009; Aula & Tienari, 2011; Puusa & Kekäle, 2013; Saarti & Juntunen, 2011; Ursin, Aittola, Henderson, & Välimaa, 2010). However, these studies have focused on describing the background of merger processes and their implementation phases in a specific university, school, or department rather than providing rigorous, systematic analyses of the impacts of mergers on research, teaching, or administrative services.

For this reason, we draw support in this section of the chapter from our empirical research on this topic in addition to other literature. Our study is based on data gathered at the beginning of the merger processes (in 2009) in six Finnish universities—Aalto University, University of Eastern Finland, University of Turku, and three member universities of the (discontinued) University Alliance (Aittola & Marttila, 2010; Ursin, Aittola, & Välimaa, 2010). The main challenges we identified were related to whether a merger was well resourced enough and whether a merger resulted in a genuine change of working practices rather than merely a poorly carried out organizational transformation. Academics feared, for example, that merger operations would take time away from their actual duties, especially from teaching and research. Some academics also worried about losing their academic identities as a consequence of a merger. This was especially the case when small units were amalgamated with larger ones. Furthermore, academics also feared that a merger would change educational practices into more "traditional" forms of teaching and learning, such as mass lectures, as well as create inflexible and bureaucratic work patterns (Ursin, Aittola, & Välimaa, 2010).

Although academics saw more challenges than possibilities in mergers, they mentioned some benefits. The main possibility raised was improvement of basic activities of merging institutions in the form of increased discussion over disciplinary and institutional borders. Academics also hoped that mergers would provide more possibilities for study arrangements and offerings for students. However, it seemed that managers and administrative staff at the merging universities were more positive about mergers than instructors and researchers, who anticipated more challenges and threats overall (Ursin, Aittola, & Välimaa, 2010).

Using a narrative perspective of analysis, Ylijoki and Ursin (2013) identified different fundamental storylines regarding how Finnish academics have reacted to various changes—especially those related to merger operations. They labeled the storylines *regressive, progressive,* and *stability.* The regressive storyline describes deterioration of work. In this storyline there is a narrative of resistance where academics relate changes to the managerialistic ideology, which is challenging to adopt. In this storyline, a merger is seen as a top–down organizational reform rather than an organic, bottom–up development. The progressive storyline, on the contrary, sees academic work moving into a more favorable direction. For example, some individual scholars, research groups, or fields of study may gain a higher position in their institutions, thereby guaranteeing immunity to or a key role in mergers. The stability storyline has a neutral stance toward changes taking place in higher education. For example, some academics may perceive that the transformations in higher education are remote, taking place at the upper levels of hierarchy with hardly any effect on their everyday lives (Ylijoki & Ursin, 2013). Clearly, academics have different interpretations on how they experience mergers. However, all view mergers as a laborious process, and if the merger is a rapid top–down process, which has been the case in Finnish universities, academics tend to commit more energy toward their everyday work than to merger operations (Puusa & Kekäle, 2013).

Discussion: Social Justice Endangered?

Mergers of HEIs have the potential to reorganize the distribution of higher education given that they may lead to the concentration of resources within a certain area (normally metropolitan) and into certain (usually the highest) social strata of students. In this regard, mergers may negatively influence social justice through limiting access to higher education and presenting challenges to equality in higher education. Seen from this perspective, mergers in Finnish higher education provide a unique view of social justice due to the broad definition of equality in Finland. According to Finnish cultural norms, every citizen—regardless of gender, ethnic background, socioeconomic background, or geographical location—should have equal opportunities to access higher education. In Finland, the fifth largest country in Western Europe and the most sparsely populated in the European Union, there has been a regional policy principle since the 1960s, which led to the establishment of a university in every province in Finland, including the most peripheral areas. This regional policy principle also determined that all Finnish universities have been developed equally, regardless of their geographical location. It has also helped to guarantee equal educational opportunities to higher education for citizens in every corner of Finland.

The ideal of equal educational opportunities can be defined in various ways, as Espinoza (2007) delineates. A conservative definition of equality emphasizes individuals' freedom to decide on their choices. A liberal perspective on equality aims to support talented students (often from high social backgrounds) as they advance in their studies, whereas a radical, or social, definition of equality is based on the idea that society guarantees both the quality of education and the equality of educational outcomes to every citizen regardless of their individual choices. According to this social definition—one that is popular in Nordic countries like Finland— the role of society is to provide equal educational opportunities and educational outcomes for every citizen, regardless of gender, socioeconomic background, or geographical location, whereas a conservative definition of equality allows society to play only a minimal role, positing that each individual should have maximal freedom to choose between educational establishments (Husén, 1972; Nori, 2011).

The social understanding of equality has influenced the goals of mergers in Finnish higher education. At the beginning of the process, one of the main goals was to create world-class universities and concentrate resources, especially within Aalto University, with the hope that it would attract top quality international faculty and students and produce a steady flow of innovations for Finnish industry. However, during the process of "structural development reform," the objective of equal educational opportunities was not forgotten in the field of Finnish higher education. This goal became quite clear in the political debate when the Finnish government tried to allocate 500 million euro extra funding specifically to Aalto University. As a result of the political process following this decision, the Finnish government found itself supporting both the establishment of world-class universities through mergers and other Finnish universities, financially as well as through the reform of Universities Act (2009). Influenced by the strong tradition of equal educational opportunities and demands to develop all Finnish universities instead of just one, the principle of equal access to higher education was not endangered.

Conclusion

From the perspective of social justice, two conclusions can be drawn from the Finnish experience with higher education mergers. First, the creation of Aalto University initially challenged the principles of equal educational opportunities and fair development of public universities, but it was balanced by the fact that all universities were eventually given more funding. Fairness and social justice were used as strong arguments to resist the concentration of resources to Finland's metropolitan area and to just one university. Second, Aalto University did ultimately receive more funding than all the other universities together because it was strongly supported by business enterprises located in the metropolitan area that is one of the economic hubs in Finland. This may, in turn, eventually lead to the creation of status hierarchies among Finnish universities. If this occurs, then the merger that resulted in Aalto University will be considered a landmark of this policy change, because traditionally the Finnish government has aimed to allocate the same amount of resources to every university, thus achieving the national goals of higher education as defined by the MoEC.

On the basis of Finland's experience with mergers, it is clear that traditions and public voice matter. Internationally, university mergers have the potential to increase social injustice because they aim to create elite universities with selective student access and faculty recruitments; however, this is not necessarily taking place in every country across the globe. Strong traditions of social justice, expressed through a desire for equal access to higher education, may act as a balancing social force.

References

Aarrevaara, T., Dobson, T. I., & Elander, C. (2009). Brave new world: Higher education reform in Finland. *Higher Education Management and Policy, 21*(2), 1–18.

Ahmadvand, A., Heidari, K., Hosseini, S. H., & Majdzadeh, R. (2012). Challenges and success factors in university mergers and academic integrations. *Archives of Iranian Medicine, 15*(12), 736–740.

Aittola, H., & Marttila, L. (Eds.). (2010). *RAKE—Yliopistojen rakenteellinen kehittäminen, akateemiset yhteisöt ja muutos. RAKE—yhteishankkeen (2008–2009) loppuraportti* [RAKE—Structural development of universities, academic communities and change. Final report of RAKE-project (2008–2009)]. Opetusministeriön julkaisuja 2010:5 [Publications of the Ministry of Education 2010:5]. Helsinki, Finland: Yliopistopaino.

Alatarvas, R. (2013). *Summary of the Finnish science barometer 2013: A study of the Finns' attitudes towards science and their opinions on scientific and technological progress.* Retrieved from http://www.tieteentiedotus.fi/files/Sciencebarometer _2013_netsummary.pdf

Aula, H. M., & Tienari, J. (2011). Becoming "world-class"? Reputation-building in a university merger. *Critical Perspectives on International Business, 7*(1), 7–29.

Bleiklie, I., & Kogan, M. (2007). Organization and governance of universities. *Higher Education Policy, 20*(4), 477–493.

5

Quality assurance is a key component of higher education systems around the world, and questions about its purpose and functions should be understood in both global and local contexts.

Questioning Quality Assurance

Kevin Kinser

Given their current ubiquity, it may be surprising to consider that formal systems of quality assurance in higher education are a fairly new phenomenon. Although the oldest systems in the United Kingdom and the United States date back more than a century, widespread adoption of accreditation in the United States occurred only in the 1950s and 1960s, and the current system in the United Kingdom was established in the 1990s. Quality assurance was not a significant part of the international higher education landscape before the mid-1980s. Over the next quarter century, however, quality assurance became a global phenomenon. In 1991, the International Network for Quality Assurance Agencies in Higher Education (INQAAHE) was founded with eight charter members. Today INQAAHE includes over 250 quality assurance agencies representing countries from Albania to Vietnam.

Several global trends served as driving forces for the expansion of quality assurance (Kinser, 2011; Sanyal & Martin, 2007; Uvalić-Trumbić, 2007). Significantly, the first is that diversification of higher education systems led to a greater variety of higher education institutions (HEIs). No longer could a sole state-sponsored university serve as the self-identified and de facto "quality beacon" for a country. Moreover, governments began expecting accountability from HEIs, particularly in response to broader political and economic demands. Quality shifted from status as an ineffable organizational feature of the university to a quantifiable response to a set of benchmarks set by external bodies.

Second, private sector institutions emerged as a global phenomenon toward the end of the 20th century (Kinser et al., 2010). When the government is the only provider of higher education, the authority of the state may be viewed as providing sufficient assurances of quality simply by its institutional sponsorship. But private sector institutions have had few claims to the historic mission of higher education. Given that these private institutions were often small, underfunded, narrowly focused on lower level

NEW DIRECTIONS FOR HIGHER EDUCATION, no. 168, Winter 2014 © 2014 Wiley Periodicals, Inc.
Published online in Wiley Online Library (wileyonlinelibrary.com) • DOI: 10.1002/he.20113

studies, and had no track record of performance, basic consumer protection required some method of determining the value of the education they purported to provide. As loan schemes and other publicly endorsed financial aid programs emerged to help students pay tuition fees, particularly in Asia and Latin America, quality assurance further developed as a way to differentiate between legitimate and illegitimate private sector institutions.

Alongside diversification of higher education, the third global trend vis-à-vis quality assurance is that demand for education from students increased. Quality assurance is one way of providing information to students and policymakers about the various choices available within a higher education marketplace. It helps to define which institutions should be considered legitimate HEIs and ensures they are offering courses and programs at sufficient levels. The high demand for education credentials can also lead some institutions to substitute academic quality for a bottom-line focus on enrollment numbers, whether or not the institution is operating as a for-profit entity. Quality assurance provides a counterweight to market pressures that can warp the mission of higher education.

A final trend that relates to the development of quality assurance as a global phenomenon is the increasing internationalization of higher education itself. National quality assurance regimes reflect the notion of educational sovereignty—that is, the right of a country to determine what educational products will be offered within its own borders. The movement of universities into foreign regulatory environments requires greater vigilance to guard against fraudulent actors taking advantage of local populations. Private institutions expanded quickly into Central and Eastern Europe after the fall of the Soviet Union, for example, because ambiguities and gaps in existing quality assurance procedures allowed weak programs to proliferate (Slantcheva & Levy, 2007). For institutions developing overseas outposts, the challenges of providing adequate oversight for activities occurring in distant locations require a robust quality assurance process that can evaluate outcomes on stated measures of performance regardless of where they occur. Internationalization of higher education means that cultural norms surrounding higher education need to be made explicit in order to facilitate entry into new markets with different traditions. Quality assurance is increasingly responsive to that demand—as in Chile, for example, where student protests against for-profit higher education led to quality assurance reviews of foreign institutions to verify compliance with excess revenue restrictions.

Defining and Mapping Key Concepts in Quality Assurance

Quality assurance can be defined in various ways. Harvey (2011) provides a comprehensive perspective by suggesting that quality assurance refers to all of the policies, procedures, and activities that are used to validate and improve the performance of an HEI. This definition includes both internal and external processes. Internal quality assurance can also be labeled as informal, in that it consists of self-defined procedures and policies that institutions use to identify and correct weaknesses in their academic programs. These are the checks and balances that operate within the university, such as procedures for shared decision making, budgetary controls, and risk management programs. External quality assurance, on the other hand, occurs as a formal process organized by an entity outside the university. These processes can be labeled as accreditation reviews, quality audits, or program assessments, and have been viewed as an accepted and expected feature of the modern era of quality assurance since the 1990s (United Nations Educational, Scientific and Cultural Organization [UNESCO], 2005). External quality assurance thus reflects the demand for accountability by outside stakeholders, as well as a neoliberal decline in trust of public service institutions seen around the world. External quality assurance may be a government-sponsored initiative, or it may be coordinated by private or nongovernmental organizations, generally with little difference in the way each form operates (Stensaker, 2013). In either case, external quality assurance is established to address broader public policy goals regarding areas such as access, affordability, economic competitiveness, and sustaining national or cultural identity.

Quality assurance relies on a shared understanding of the meaning of "quality" in higher education (van Ginkel & Dias, 2007). Scholars have articulated three ways to define quality (Sanyal & Martin, 2007). First, quality is represented by fitness *for* purpose, in which high-quality education fulfills its own self-stated objectives. This recognizes and celebrates the diversity of educational missions, emphasizing that educational leaders internally determine the HEI's mission. A remote higher education outpost may be more aligned with teaching practical skills, for example, and thus fulfill a different mission than a world-class research university—but the outpost can still be high quality in meeting its mission based on its unique objectives in the local environment.

Quality may also be represented by fitness *of* purpose. This view refers to the insistence that education should be relevant to objectives defined by the local society, the classic "education for the public good" argument. In this representation of quality, high-quality higher education must be about more than meeting objectives as defined by the university, or even by the individual. It must benefit the society as a whole, and must therefore be externally imposed and evaluated by society—ideally keeping in mind concerns of the local context.

Finally, a more practical, standards-based model for understanding quality involves determining whether education achieves explicitly stated criteria for performance. Quality is therefore often defined by indicators rather than measured directly. This is an oft-criticized model of quality assurance, especially when the indicators evaluate quality based on resources and other inputs, rather than the outcomes of education (Gaston, 2013). This model nevertheless remains quite common, with outcome-focused modifications in the United States, for example, requiring measurable student learning and demonstration of competencies as indicators of institutional quality (Krzykowski & Kinser, 2014).

Quality Assurance Functions

Quality assurance in education has two primary functions. The first function is to establish the legitimacy of an educational program. The second is to serve as a source of information about the purpose and outcomes of the program for decision makers.

Legitimacy through quality assurance procedures may make a program eligible for government support or it may serve as a signal to students that the education provided has some extrinsic worth. According to organizational theorists, legitimacy can be evaluated in several different ways (Suchman, 1995). It can be based on the practical value that an organization has to a particular group of constituents, or can come from adopting an organizational form that is widely viewed as legitimate. Legitimacy can also be attributed to organizations that engage in activities that are the "right thing to do" and benefit the community. No matter what form legitimacy takes, it is important to understand that the source of legitimacy is always external to the organization itself (Suchman, 1995). In other words, legitimacy is something that is granted by a community, suggesting that when the community changes, the conditions for legitimacy also change. Quality assurance standards, therefore, represent the expectations of the external community that is evaluating educational practice. Obtaining formal legitimacy via quality assurance procedures is crucial for conveying to the public the fundamental credibility and acceptability of the degree by certifying a baseline of legitimacy.

Quality assurance also functions as a source of information about education necessary for decision makers. Students and their families may use quality assurance reports and indicators, when available, to evaluate which program will best meet their needs. Data on criteria made public through quality assurance reviews, such as graduation rates, instructor credentials, or technology support, may be relevant for program selection or determining whether the education would be a good investment in time and resources for a prospective student. For those in government, quality assurance can be a way to compel HEIs to measure and disclose details about their operations that are important for policy. For example, a quality assurance standard that requires authentic measures of student learning can be used to guide the distribution of funds for institutional improvement. Regulators can use other accreditation standards on admissions or academic progress to enforce professional standards of practice.

Types of Quality Assurance

Quality assurance can be applied to the institution or educational provider or to the individual program. Less frequently, quality assurance may be applied at the course level. When quality assurance targets the provider, analysts consider the internal checks and oversight at the institution across all academic efforts. Often the focus is on organizational support, infrastructure, and resources necessary to provide education of a specific type, or at a specific level. Because of this, institutional quality assurance may look different depending on the goals and mission of the HEI. For example, quality assurance for a university may require examination of research labs and faculty publications to determine whether a program of study is adequately supported. A technical training institution, on the other hand, may focus on the experience of the faculty in industry or the equipment used to train students. It is inappropriate, therefore, to compare quality among institutions of different types.

Quality assurance of individual programs involves evaluating the specifics of a program of study against standards set by a professional body or government. For academic programs, reviews by officials or peers ensure that the program has an up-to-date curriculum and adequate criteria for completion or certification. For other programs, such as those that prepare students for entry-level work or advancement in a specific industry or profession, a professional association or group of current leaders in the field often sets the evaluative criteria. Sometimes the criteria are endorsed by government agencies, such that licensure to practice is dependent on acceptable quality as determined by the profession.

Course-based quality assurance is not common, mostly because it is a labor-intensive activity for external reviewers to attempt. This activity generally falls under the rubric of internal quality assurance, where the institution itself provides direct oversight over its courses. Course-based quality assurance may be accomplished directly by the instructor of record or may involve managers and supervisors reviewing course materials to ensure that they meet program goals and organizational guidelines. Competency-based education can also be viewed as a form of course-based quality assurance. In this model, learning outcomes for a course are framed as competencies to be demonstrated. An external evaluator determines whether the student is competent in the areas covered by the learning outcomes. The competency evaluation can be ratcheted up to the program level by accumulating competency endorsements. This model is still relatively rare, but has received traction in recent years due to the potential and scalability of technology-based assessments (see, e.g., U.S. Department of Education, n.d.).

In addition to categorizing quality assurance based on its focus on institutions, programs, or courses, the quality assurance process can also be grouped into several categories or models. The *accreditation* model of quality assurance provides a summative evaluation to determine whether or not an educational program or HEI should continue in its present form. Typically, a negative accreditation review precipitates closure or other dramatic restructuring of the program or HEI. The *assessment* model of quality assurance evaluates how good a program is and offers feedback for improvement. This model assumes a quality improvement perspective, where the goal of quality assurance is to identify weaknesses and correct them. A third type of quality assurance is the *ranking* model. The goal here is to use a series of indicators to comprehensively evaluate a program or institution against other similarly situated entities. Shanghai Jiao Tong University's *Academic Rankings of World Universities*, for example, provides an international evaluation of the quality of research universities around the world. Governments may do something similar within their countries using league tables that place institutions in categories for funding or additional subsidies—a topic Ellen Hazelkorn discusses in Chapter 2 of this volume. Models are often combined, as with an accreditation process that involves an expectation of continuous quality improvement.

Quality Assurance Standards

Standards are the language through which quality assurance agencies communicate their expectations to institutions and the public. They are at once normative statements and aspirational value judgments in the sense that they represent what "ought" to be the case and are ideally realizable by all programs.

Quality assurance standards reflect the philosophy of education that predominates in a given country. For example, the United States values institutional autonomy, decentralized oversight, and academic freedom; these values are embedded in the standards employed. Other countries have recently changed their systems and have developed strategies designed to confront problems incurred under earlier systems. For example, Australia originally had nine separate agencies at the national and state levels with quality assurance responsibilities for the country's universities. The new Tertiary Education Quality and Standards Agency (TEQSA) was designed to unify various agencies under a common set of threshold standards. Other systems reflect the unique evolution of the higher education system and adapt their quality assurance procedures to address specific needs. The Dubai Free Zone (DFZ) model, for instance, is a case where quality assurance of foreign universities is the dominant concern. Dubai created a quality assurance model that relies on evidence of appropriate oversight from the home country and home campus rather than duplicating the effort locally for the international branch campuses located in the DFZ.

Quality assurance standards might be viewed as a local solution to the problem of ensuring that higher education is of sufficient quality to meet the needs of students and society at large. There is no cookie-cutter model that can be employed across multiple jurisdictions without consideration of the local context. Quality assurance standards should therefore ideally emerge out of a consensus dialogue with the communities most directly affected by the quality assurance process, and standards will vary accordingly. They might be threshold standards, like those in the Australian model. They might be representations of quality through identifying ideal characteristics of HEIs and programs, as in the UK system. Alternatively, they might focus on institutional mission, allowing institutions to self-identify their goals and assess how well they meet them, which is largely how things are done in the United States.

Standards also reflect input and output criteria. On the one hand, it is important to know that the basic infrastructure is sufficient to support high-quality education. Adequate buildings, staffing, and scholarship must be in place before students arrive in order to justify the approval of a program of study. On the other hand, even the best infrastructure cannot by itself produce actual learning and competent graduates—it requires the interaction of students and the curriculum, moderated by the faculty and other subject matter experts, and evaluated through authentic assessments of outcomes.

Finally, standards encompass the tension between consistency and innovation. They are bureaucratic rules that must be followed, with exceptions violating the very notion of a standard of quality. At the same time, they are often put in place to address innovation and new educational opportunities. Standards must recognize where the letter of the law gets in the way of the purpose for the rule. On this last point, accreditation is especially vulnerable to critique. Indeed, both the United States and Australia are currently engaged in a debate about the ability of quality assurance regulations to protect against poor quality while welcoming innovations that may potentially improve the system (Baird, 2013; Krzykowski & Kinser, 2014). The United States in particular faces this debate regularly, with cycles of increased flexibility in standards leading critics to blame loose regulation for the problematic outcomes that follow. The standards therefore tighten again to place certain activities out of bounds. New developments inevitably push the boundaries of the revised quality assurance regulations, and soon critics want more regulatory flexibility again in the name of facilitating innovation. Thus, it is important that standards are regularly reviewed with an eye toward accommodating promising innovation without opening the floodgates to unscrupulous providers.

Questioning Quality Assurance

Since medieval times, institutions of higher education have been trusted to do what is in the public interest. Quality assurance reflects the modern ambiguity of that trust. The metaphor of "knights and knaves" in public service, which Le Grand (2003, 2007) first suggested in his work on policy implementation, is critical in understanding this ambiguity. Are public servants "knights" who sacrifice themselves to nobly fulfill the public mission, or are they "knaves" who act only out of self-interest and will contradict the public mission if they see an advantage to doing so?

The dual model for quality assurance involving both internal and external mechanisms in use around the world can be interpreted via this metaphor. On the one hand, the weight given to internal quality assurance mechanisms and higher education autonomy assumes that HEIs are made up of knights who can be trusted for their intrinsic motivation and noble pursuit of the truth. Under this model, all HEIs seek to be high quality and will naturally design internal procedures to maintain their reputations and value propositions. On the other hand, most recent policies insist on external quality assessments due to well-founded mistrust about the motivations of the knaves that populate HEIs. To make sure that their knavish self-interest is kept under control, quality must be validated by outside stakeholders.

To be sure, quality assurance is not value neutral. It is, in fact, a process that reflects values inherent in higher education. Because these values are not universally shared, and reflect contested issues of national identity, political structure, and status within the global economic community of nations, quality assurance should be questioned even as it becomes nearly universal in its application. What is the purpose of quality assurance? Who are its constituents? Who determines the standards and how are they measured? The answers to these questions can illuminate the values of the higher education systems that quality assurance is designed to protect.

The Purpose of Quality Assurance.   Not only is quality a contested concept in higher education, but it is also a relatively new one. The tension between tradition and innovation means that quality can be achieved by replicating existing structures, just as new structures can build quality by correcting problems in the old systems. Globalization can threaten quality inherent in local institutions, or it can serve as an exhibit for "world-class" standards. Western models of quality assurance that have served as global exemplars suggest the value of independent quality assessments to guard against weak performance and fraudulent activities. However, some countries have shown a much greater interest in protecting their educational sovereignty from foreign encroachment. China, for example, has set up an entire regulatory system for Sino-foreign cooperation in education based on the understanding that all partnerships are Chinese-led and based on Chinese priorities. Other countries—like Australia—see quality assurance as a way of emphasizing standards to which all HEIs should aspire. Finally, models exist that reflect regional interests in the mobility of educational credentials, so standardization among various systems is viewed as "what matters." This is suggested by the goal of harmonization of regional policies among many Southeast Asian countries and the model for the quality assurance principles of the European Higher Education Area (EHEA). A global system of quality assurance needs to serve multiple purposes and reflect the national, subnational, and international interests that guide its formation.

NEW DIRECTIONS FOR HIGHER EDUCATION • DOI: 10.1002/he

education where the host country must assume responsibility for quality of the foreign higher education outpost, regardless of its origin. Some regional models, such as those sponsored by the Association of Southeast Asian Nations or the European Union, seek to harmonize quality assurance so that it has similar meaning across borders. However, these are stop-gap measures. It is clear that multinational quality assurance does not exist, even as the multinational university is becoming more common.

The second issue follows from the first. If the problem is inadequate procedures in some countries, then the export of established quality assurance standards should be welcomed. In other words, the presumptive "gold standard" models used in the United States or the United Kingdom could frame new systems in nations like Uzbekistan or Iraq. Indeed, officials hoping to replicate well-established quality assurance systems often recruit advisors from countries that have successfully developed robust policies. As noted several times in this chapter, however, the standards and processes for quality assurance should nonetheless reflect local settings, culture, and history. It is the local dimensions of education that provide its vitality and relevance to the local population. This is where educational sovereignty and the standardization of quality assurance ought to come together. Certain principles of quality assurance have cross-cultural dimensions (UNESCO, 2005), such as transparency in standards and consistency in their application. These principles can perhaps form the basis for improving quality assurance alongside local needs and, by implication, improve higher education.

The third challenge is the role of technology in higher education and how that can impact quality assurance procedures. As is the case in so many other industries around the world, the ability of technology to allow HEIs to collect voluminous amounts of data applies to quality assurance data collection as well. Particularly with the expansion of online learning, data on student–faculty interactions and the documentation of learning outcomes have become more routine. Internal human resource databases can track employees from the moment of application through retirement. As these data points are linked with other data, a new form of "Big Data" emerges. Big Data can provide a rich source of information about the operations of education providers that were formerly invisible, and can serve as the source for unobtrusive measures that may make the reporting function for organizations less onerous. At the same time, Big Data puts more responsibility on the capacity of the quality assurance agency to use the information wisely and protect the security of the information it has received. This is a new front for quality assurance, one that will likely rise in importance in the years to come.

Finally, the larger debate about higher education as a tradable service will impact the design of emergent global quality assurance regimes. Since the General Agreement on Trade in Services (GATS) was created in 1995, education has been on the negotiating table, treated no differently from other industries (Bassett, 2006). Questions about educational sovereignty, however, have regularly scuttled attempts to formulate a broad, multilateral agreement to open countries' borders to foreign investment in the education sector. However, bilateral agreements can be developed that create structures of trust between two countries with mutually secure quality assurance regimes (Lane & Kinser, 2013). These reciprocity agreements could facilitate cross-border mobility while providing a model for broader arrangements between trusted partners. These arrangements rely on a robust and reliable quality assurance process—one that few countries can claim to have at this point.

The global mobility of students, staff, curriculum, and institutions contributes to an international market for higher education. Yet quality assurance remains local in its regulatory standing, with no true transnational models currently in existence. Most quality assurance agencies are government-controlled or endorsed, and countries have been understandably reluctant to relinquish their sovereignty in this matter to an outside entity. There are therefore tensions between local and global priorities, and the values reflected in sustaining the "public good" across cultures are not universally shared.

The priority in initial development of quality assurance systems was to protect the integrity of the national system; what happened beyond borders was an afterthought. Now, however, global competition for resources, students, and faculty requires a quality assurance regime that can navigate borders and boundaries without sacrificing closely held academic values and local customs and needs. This remains the challenge for quality assurance in the decades to come.

References

Baird, J. (2013). TEQSA and risk-based regulation. *Australian Universities' Review, 55*(2), 72–79.

Bassett, R. M. (2006). *The WTO and the university: Globalization, GATS, and American higher education* (Studies in Higher Education). New York, NY: Routledge.

Carey, K. (2010, March/April). Asleep at the seal: Just how bad does a college have to be to lose accreditation? *Washington Monthly*. Retrieved from http://www.washingtonmonthly.com/features/2010/1003.carey.html

Gaston, P. (2013). *Higher education accreditation: How it's changing, why it must.* Sterling, VA: Stylus.

Harvey, L. (2011, March 19). *Analytical quality glossary* (Quality Research International). Retrieved from www.qualityresearchinternational.com/glossary/

Heller, D. E., & Callender, C. (2013). *Student financing of higher education: A comparative perspective.* New York, NY: Routledge.

Kinser, K. (2011). Quality assurance in cross-border higher education. In J. E. Lane & K. Kinser (Eds.), *Multinational colleges and universities: Leading, governing, and managing international branch campuses* (pp. 53–64). San Francisco, CA: Jossey-Bass.

Kinser, K., Levy, D. C., Silas, J. C., Bernasconi, A., Slantcheve-Durst, S., Otieno, W., . . . LaSota, R. (2010). *The global growth of private higher education: ASHE Higher Education Report Series* (Vol. 36, No. 3). San Francisco, CA: Wiley.

Krzykowski, L., & Kinser, K. (2014, May/June). Transparency in student learning assessment: Can accreditation standards make a difference? *Change: The Magazine of Higher Learning, 46*(3), 67–73.

Lane, J. E., & Kinser, K. (2013, August 6). Solving the regulatory challenges of international campuses. *The Chronicle of Higher Education.* Retrieved from http://chronicle.com/blogs/worldwise/solving-the-regulatory-challenges-of-international-campuses/32515

Le Grand, J. (2003). *Motivation, agency, and public policy: Of knights and knaves, pawns and queens.* Oxford, UK: Oxford University Press.

Le Grand, J. (2007). *The other invisible hand: Delivering public services through choice and competition.* Oxford, UK: Princeton University Press.

Loofbourow, L. (2013, May 16). "Not to profit": Fighting privatization in Chile. *Boston Review.* Retrieved from http://bostonreview.net/world/%E2%80%9Cno-profit %E2%80%9D

Sanyal, B. C., & Martin, M. (2007). Quality assurance and the role of accreditation: An overview. In Global University Network for Innovation (Ed.), *Higher education in the world 2007: Accreditation for quality assurance: What is at stake?* (pp. 3–17). New York, NY: Palgrave Macmillan.

Slantcheva, S., & Levy, D. C. (Eds.). (2007). *In search of legitimacy: Private higher education in Central and Eastern Europe.* New York, NY: Palgrave Macmillan.

Stensaker, B. (2013). External quality auditing. Strengths and shortcomings in the audit process. In M. Shah & C. Sid Nair (Eds.), *External quality audit. Has it improved quality assurance in universities?* (pp. 195–207). Cambridge, UK: Woodhead.

Suchman, M. C. (1995). Managing legitimacy: Strategic and institutional approaches. *Academy of Management Journal, 20*(3), 571–610.

United Nations Educational, Scientific and Cultural Organization. (2005). *Guidelines for quality provision in cross-border higher education.* Paris, France: Author.

U.S. Department of Education. (n.d.). *Competency-based learning or personalized learning.* Retrieved from http://www.ed.gov/oii-news/competency-based-learning -or-personalized-learning

Uvalić-Trumbić, S. (2007). The international politics of quality assurance and accreditation: From legal instruments to communities of practice. In Global University Network for Innovation (Ed.), *Higher education in the world 2007: Accreditation for quality assurance: What is at stake?* (pp. 58–72). New York, NY: Palgrave Macmillan.

van Ginkel, H. J. A., & Dias, M. A. R. (2007). Institutional and political challenges of accreditation at the international level. In Global University Network for Innovation (Ed.), *Higher education in the world 2007: Accreditation for quality assurance: What is at stake?* (pp. 37–57). New York, NY: Palgrave Macmillan.

KEVIN KINSER *is an associate professor and senior researcher in the Institute for Global Education Policy Studies at the State University of New York at Albany.*

6

In this chapter, the authors explore various types of cross-border higher education, considering equity and quality issues within these developments. With a particular focus on international branch campuses, the authors discuss the ways in which global competition for knowledge and economic development interact with tensions at the local level.

Cross-Border Higher Education: Global and Local Tensions Within Competition and Economic Development

Taya L. Owens, Jason E. Lane

The world of higher education is buzzing about competition. The pursuit of enhanced prestige, greater student market share, and new resources is affecting higher education across the globe, with much of the discourse focusing on competition among higher education institutions (HEIs). Higher education has become part of a broader competitive landscape among nations, one in which knowledge and knowledge makers play an increasingly significant role in the economic and political success of a country (Lane, 2012; Wildavsky, 2010).

Indeed, the economic discourse in higher education has changed markedly over the last two decades. The changes are due in part to an increased perception that earning a college degree contributes to an individual's quality of life. Government policies frequently link economic competitiveness to the capacity of a nation's workforce and the strength of its higher education system (Carnevale & Rose, 2012; Lane & Owens, 2012). Moreover, colleges and universities have realized that the higher education market is now global, that competition for students is intensifying, and that prestige is tied to both the breadth and depth of an institution's global footprint (Altbach, Reisberg, & Rumbley, 2009). Private providers increasingly offer substantial shares of advanced education and training, representing a marked shift in some nations where higher education had almost exclusively been the purview of the public realm (Levy, 2006; McBurnie & Ziguras, 2007). Amid the expansion of globalization and privatization

New Directions for Higher Education, no. 168, Winter 2014 © 2014 Wiley Periodicals, Inc.
Published online in Wiley Online Library (wileyonlinelibrary.com) • DOI: 10.1002/he.20114

forces, cross-border higher education (CBHE)—the specific focus of this chapter—has proliferated.

Internationalization in higher education has traditionally referred to sending students and faculty abroad or bringing the world to the HEI campus through foreign student recruitment and cross-cultural curricular experiences. Over the past several decades, other forms of internationalization have emerged, wherein academic programs, research initiatives, and capacity building assistance have moved across international borders (Knight, 2004; Lane & Kinser, 2011; McBurnie & Ziguras, 2007). These activities have been broadly labeled "transnational education," "offshoring," and "cross-border higher education"; in this chapter, we use the latter term to describe this phenomenon. These efforts have not occurred in a vacuum; they are part of a broader set of movements related to growing competition in higher education, as described throughout this volume. The story of CBHE is not just about the growing competition within higher education, however. A closer look reveals that trends in CBHE reflect a growing economic and diplomatic competition between nations—a competition driven by the pursuit of knowledge and those who produce it.

The rapid development of cross-border higher education comes at a time when knowledge has emerged as an important influence in both the global economy and economic competition among nations. This is not a recent realization. More than four decades ago, Clark Kerr (1963) observed, "We are just now perceiving that the university's invisible product, knowledge, may be the most powerful single element in our culture, affecting the rise and fall of professions and even of social classes, of regions, and even of nations" (pp. xi–xii). What is different today is an increased global awareness of the economic and diplomatic importance of higher education. Beyond the academy, national governments are investing in and competing for status within the higher education sector. In fact, the importance of knowledge to national economies and societies has positioned HEIs as important actors in the competition between nations, which Wildavsky (2010) coined "the great brain race."

The rapid expansion of CBHE in the midst of rising global competition for knowledge often masks important tensions at the local level. Although a certain level of academic analysis focuses on increases in student and scholarly mobility alongside academic programs and institutions moving between nations, what is often overlooked in the related discourse are "the ways in which local sites and their histories, cultures, politics and pedagogies mediate to greater or lesser extents the effects of top-down globalization" (Rizvi & Lingard, 2010, p. 65). The purpose of this chapter is to describe the various types of CBHE, considering equity and quality issues therein, and to explore the ways in which competition for knowledge is driving CBHE development, while unpacking the tensions that reveal themselves at the local level.

Types of Cross-Border Higher Education

Cross-border education encompasses situations where people, programs, or providers move across national jurisdictional borders (Knight, 2003). These groups serve nicely to frame the dimensions of international mobility; however, it is important to note that these different groupings often take place together. For example, when programs are established overseas, home country faculty relocate at least temporarily to help set up these new programs. Similarly, program mobility is often accompanied by a foreign education outpost or some type of institutional mobility. In this section, we highlight four facets of CBHE—students, faculty, programs, and institutions—and discuss potential equity issues that arise within each type of cross-border higher education.

Students.   Currently, just over four million students are enrolled in a degree program at an HEI in another country (Organisation for Economic Co-operation and Development [OECD], 2013). The number of students crossing borders for advanced educational training has increased steadily over the past several decades, mirroring the expansion of students enrolling in higher education programs. The increase in these numbers shows no signs of abating; estimates have placed total international student mobility at just over 7 million by 2025 (Böhm, Davis, Meares, & Pearce, 2002). There are some notable patterns among these 4 million students. Half of all students, about 2 million, come from an Asian country, with students from China, Korea, and India making up a considerable amount of the total. A second large group of international students includes European citizens swirling through the European Union, the majority of whom participate in programs inspired by the regional mobility policies in the European Higher Education Area (EHEA).

Approximately 3 million international students enroll at a campus in an OECD member nation; the most popular destinations continue to be English-speaking countries. The United States has historically been the most popular destination country, followed by the United Kingdom and Australia. However, patterns of global mobility appear to have shifted in the past 10 years. Although the United States still hosts the largest numbers of students, the overall percentage of international students studying in the United States has decreased. Students are starting to select other countries for study abroad. In fact, in 2011 about 8% of students known to be studying abroad, or just over 320,000 students, chose to study in China.

In addition, international exchange and harmonization frameworks, such as the Bologna Process between European countries, are spurring growth in student and faculty mobility. Similarly, in Asia, the Association of South East Asian Nations (ASEAN) has begun to coordinate Asian countries as they take their first steps toward more widespread mobility. The ASEAN regional higher education frameworks are designed to facilitate

NEW DIRECTIONS FOR HIGHER EDUCATION • DOI: 10.1002/he

students pursuing international study experiences within the region (Lohani, 2013; McDermott, 2014).

Equity in Student Mobility.   Who has access to higher education? These overall trends in expanding global mobility mask some fundamental disparities between students who have access to studying abroad and those who do not. Overall student access to higher education has not developed uniformly across the globe and neither has access to study abroad opportunities. Global student flows continue to be marked by regional and socioeconomic disparities. For example, participation rates in sub-Saharan Africa and parts of Latin America and the Caribbean continue to lag behind those of more developed or emerging economies (OECD, 2013). Tuition and fees for international students represent prohibitive costs for students with meager financial resources. In certain cultures, particularly in the Middle East and Asia, women are prohibited from traveling abroad without an escort, making study abroad more accessible to male students than females. Within the United States, those studying abroad tend to be White, female, and have access to financial wealth, resulting in disproportionately fewer students of color pursuing such opportunities (Picard, Bernardino, & Ehigiator, 2009).

Faculty.   As the primary guardians of academic programs and course design, faculty occupy a central position within CBHE. Faculty may engage in cross-border activities in a myriad of ways, ranging from limited visits (such as those sponsored by Fulbright or other nationally funded exchange programs) to pursuing academic careers outside of their countries of origin. Case studies on faculty involvement in internationalization have suggested that about 40% of U.S. faculty consider their teaching and research to include a cross-border dimension; otherwise, they view their work as directly involved in study abroad programs (Dewey & Duff, 2009). Just as some U.S. faculty are incorporating global dimensions into their professional portfolios, the U.S. academic labor force is becoming more international. As of 2006, the National Science Foundation reported that 20% of all full-time faculty at U.S. institutions were foreign born, with more than half of full-time faculty and academic researchers in computer science coming from outside the United States (National Science Board, 2010).

The Careers of Doctorate Holders (CDH), a collaborative project administered and managed by OECD, the United Nations Educational, Scientific and Cultural Organization (UNESCO) Institute for Statistics, and Eurostat, provides perhaps the only large-scale international data collection on this topic. On average, 14% of doctorate holders from a mostly European sample of 25 countries reported working abroad in the previous 10 years (Auriol, Misu, & Freeman, 2013). The majority of doctorate holders circulated within Europe and the United States. Most spent less than a year working abroad and perhaps only traveled once during the 10 years under review in the study. In some countries, however, doctorate holders moved between countries more frequently (Hungary, Bulgaria, Romania) and stayed longer once they arrived (Portugal, Spain, Malta). The majority of doctorate holders cited academic factors as the main impetus for international mobility, as compared to other motivations such as job opportunities or personal, economic, or political reasons (Auriol et al., 2013). Although many faculty find that a period spent abroad is helpful to their careers, the great majority are still focused on a career at home. National labor markets and national career structures continue to exert considerable influence in faculty mobility.

Equity in Faculty Conditions.   Are faculty at foreign outposts provided with fair working conditions? Although little research has been produced on this topic, the field broadly acknowledges that inequities related to gender, ethnicity, discipline, and location do appear in terms of faculty working conditions in CBHE. Such inequities can influence the experiences of faculty who choose to work outside of their home countries. The UNESCO *Recommendation Concerning the Status of Higher Education Teaching Personnel* (UNESCO, 1997) established a baseline of norms and standards for educators working in colleges and universities. The recommendation directly addresses working conditions and terms of service, collegial governance, and academic freedom. Nevertheless, a formal international mechanism to ensure that campuses are providing their faculty with these rights and freedoms does not yet exist.

Curricular Programs.   Curricula travel across borders through various modes, all of which require different organizational structures and agreements between multiple parties. Cross-border curriculum transfer consists of five potential core models (Knight, 2006a): franchise, articulation, joint degrees, distance education, and international branch campuses (IBCs); IBCs will be considered separately in the section on institutions later. A franchise is a CBHE agreement whereby an HEI in Country A allows a campus in Country B to offer its curriculum in Country B. The degree is awarded by the campus in Country A, offering students a program of study leading to an authentic degree from a licensed college or university situated in another country. Arrangements for administration, management, teaching, cost assessment, and academic credit are customized for each franchising agreement; these agreements comply with national regulations of the host country (Alderman, 2001).

In articulation, or twinning, CBHE agreements, students gain credit for courses and programs offered by other collaborating partners. This arrangement allows students to gain credit for work done at another campus, though the campus where the student completes the final stages of the program usually awards the degree (Daniel, Kanwar, & Uvalic-Trumbic, 2005). Joint degree arrangements in CBHE consist of two providers collaborating to offer a program for which a student either receives one joint award from both campuses or two degrees (one from each campus). Partnering institutions customize provisions of these programs for awarding qualifications, operating in accordance with regulations and laws of each country (Knight,

2006b). Finally, distance education describes a CBHE arrangement where a provider delivers courses or a program to students in other countries through distance and online modes that may include face-to-face instruction and support for students through local study or support centers (van der Wende, 2003).

Equity in Curricular Quality.   Is the curriculum appropriate? Is the curriculum consistent? Historically, curricula reflected a largely local influence, occasionally adapted to incorporate outside influences. Frank and Gabler (2006) documented global shifts in curricular offerings, shifts influenced by Western institutional norms and values. This importing of curricula has raised concerns about the differences between foreign and indigenous curricula, prompting unease about the influence of a dominant global curriculum. As a response to this concern, some authors from the Global South have suggested that there is space for local curriculum in global models, suggesting ways of incorporating traditional concepts and pedagogy into modern programs (Kanu, 2007).

Beyond a host campus adopting a foreign curriculum, some foreign institutions offer courses or programs in overseas locations. In such situations, program directors often debate whether the curriculum should remain standardized across locations or be adapted to local expectations, and what the implications might be of this adaptation in curricular quality. Within the context of CBHE, "quality" is most commonly defined as offering higher education that is equivalent or comparable to what is offered in the home country (Coleman, 2003; Ip, 2006; Kinser, 2011; McBurnie & Ziguras, 2007; Stella, 2006); see Chapter 5 in this volume for further discussion on this topic. Government agencies, accreditation boards, and home institutions have raised concerns about program quality, including the use of short-term faculty and faculty with low-level credentials, as well as low admission standards for students (Lim, 2009). On the other hand, nations such as the United Kingdom and Australia have been particularly active in evolving their efforts to assure the quality of CBHE offered by their institutions.

Institutions.   An international branch campus is an "entity that is owned, at least in part, by a foreign education provider; operated in the name of the foreign education provider; engages in at least some face-to-face teaching; and provides access to an entire academic program that leads to a credential awarded by the foreign education provider" (Lane, 2011, p. 5). International branch campuses may be wholly owned by the home campus, operated in partnership with a foreign investor, or subsidized by the host government (Lane, 2010; Lane & Kinser, 2011). Currently, about 200 campuses have set up IBCs overseas, nearly half of which U.S. institutions operate (C-BERT, 2014). Most other IBCs are linked to home campuses in the United Kingdom and Australia. Although the majority of U.S. home campuses are private, the majority of non-U.S. home campuses are public. That being said, all IBCs are considered private in the country of operation, even if they receive public subsidies (Lane & Kinser, 2011). The most popular programs offered are professional; the Master of Business Administration continues to be the most popular degree by enrollment.

Equity in Institutional Mission. Do foreign outposts offer the same public service to the host country that home campuses provide to their local communities? One of the main criticisms leveraged at IBCs has been the apparent "gold rush" mentality of seeking knowledge for money's sake rather than knowledge for truth's sake. Research has suggested that campuses with a gold rush mentality tend not to last very long, whereas those IBCs that have integrated with the host government along several dimensions contribute to the public purposes and needs of the local community and host country (Lane & Kinser, 2011). In recent research, Kinser and Lane (2013) distinguished between IBCs *being* capacity versus *building* capacity. Building capacity requires close attention to the needs of the host country, especially in terms of what existing capacity is already in place. This requires engaging in educational activities that are locally relevant and determined by local government and community goals and requirements. Some initial evidence indicates that as IBCs age and become more locally embedded, many begin to pursue locally relevant research agendas and even consult with and build capacity in domestic institutions.

Key Players and Motivations for Cross-Border Higher Education

Unlike domestic higher education, where an institution operates in only one country, CBHE by its very nature involves at least two countries and at least two governments (Lane & Kinser, 2011). Thus, to fully understand cross-border higher education and related critiques, it is important to understand its development from multiple perspectives. For the purposes of the remainder of this chapter, we focus explicitly on the development of IBCs for two reasons. First, the limits of this chapter preclude a more in-depth analysis of these issues across the various forms of CBHE. Second, multiple key players—namely home institutions, importing countries, and exporting countries—are more likely to be actively engaged in the development of an IBC. Although we focus on these three dominant players, important state or regional governments and agencies play important roles in some cases.

Home Institutions. There are a number of internal factors pushing institutions to open cross-border branches—namely resources, regulation, and reputation. As mentioned previously, the majority of the foreign education providers that set up branch campuses come from a Western nation. In light of declining government subsidies at home, concerns about rising tuition rates, and heightened competition for students, some colleges and universities look for new ways to expand their reach. In addition, campuses often perceive an opportunity for innovation in a different country, where the rules and regulations of the home nation do not constrain innovative

NEW DIRECTIONS FOR HIGHER EDUCATION • DOI: 10.1002/he

efforts. Finally, global engagement seems to be increasingly tied to an institution's reputation. Opening foreign outposts may be seen as a signal of a strong resource base or high demand for an institution's academic programs.

However, the reasons that foster such expansion do not always align with reality, as illustrated by the recent retreats of the overseas expansions of George Mason University, Michigan State University, and the University of LaVerne. These campuses, like other failed branches, closed because they either encountered unexpected market and cultural conditions or lacked sufficient support from the home campus. Unrealistic projections of revenue and enrollment, regulatory conflicts, and incompatible partnerships are the hallmarks of a bungled branch.

IBC operations and setup are complicated by a different set of laws, cultural expectations, and local educational infrastructure (Harding & Lammey, 2011). Abu Dhabi is very different from New York City, which is very different from Shanghai. Moreover, as pioneers in an educational experiment, faculty and staff may be called on to help with a variety of tasks including budget planning, recruiting students, course scheduling, website design, furniture construction, staffing residence halls, and fixing computers—tasks that do not normally fall into the domain of their job expectations at home.

Importing Countries.   Receiving nations often invest in IBCs with the hope of building national educational capacity, strengthening workforce development, or enhancing research and innovation. The established infrastructure of a campus in one country is repurposed in another country with the intention of educating students, fostering local research and innovation, and, through spillover, improving the overall quality of the domestic education sector. Some importing nations have sought to raise their own international reputations by aligning themselves with well-respected institutions such as Duke, Yale, and Texas A&M (Lane, 2010). In a related development, HEIs have occasionally become tools of public diplomacy. Some importing governments see IBCs as a means to strengthen their alliances with the exporting nations or vice versa.

Many countries have developed strategies and enacted policies to encourage IBC development through an education hub. The precise schemata of educational hubs remains somewhat ambiguous (see Knight's chapter in this volume), though they have rhetorical power in the education plans of countries like Malaysia and South Korea (Kinser & Lane, 2010; Knight, 2011). Hubs usually indicate a country's intention to promote itself as a regional or international destination for students. In the IBC context, hubs further imply that foreign HEIs will form a significant part of local educational capacity. Places like Qatar and the United Arab Emirates' Abu Dhabi have provided financial and regulatory incentives to attract prestigious IBCs. However, the most popular of destinations, Dubai, offers no direct subsidy; in fact, IBCs are charged high rents to operate in places such as the Dubai International Academic City. Foreign universities have demonstrated interest in locating branches near rapidly expanding academic markets. It is no accident that most of the IBCs built in the past decade are located around the Indian Ocean and Pacific Rim.

Exporting Countries. Whereas home institutions and importing countries are actively involved in IBC operations, exporting countries engage in IBC development to varying degrees. Some nations, such as the United States, play little formal role in campus activities. A recent review of CBHE policies within the 50 states in the United States revealed that few state governments paid any attention to the activities of their public institutions outside of their state—so long as state funds were not used to support out-of-state activity (Lane, Kinser, & Knox, 2012). From our gathering of anecdotal data and information from the "gray" (or more informally published) literature, it appears that many nations currently take a similar laissez-faire approach to the work of their campuses outside their borders. At the other end of the continuum, Australia and increasingly the United Kingdom have developed an active policy agenda that supports and regulates IBC development. Both nations have recognized that CBHE is an important strategy for advancing the economic and political interests of their institutions and the nation as a whole. In fact, HEIs in both nations now educate more international students in their offshore activities than within their home borders. Australia has been active in promoting and branding their domestic and international higher education activities; they have also established regulations prohibiting the use of government funds overseas. At the time of this writing, the United Kingdom was actively exploring whether government funding should be used to support the development of international branch campuses.

Contested Campuses: Global Trends, Local Forces

In more recent years, several high-profile international branch campus dissolutions have prompted professional and academic calls for caution. Branches have closed for reasons ranging from the preventable, such as insufficient market research before engaging in high-risk investments, to the unexpected, such as breakdowns in partner negotiation, to the eventual, such as successful achievement of a predetermined goal. In 2009, the Observatory of Borderless Higher Education (OBHE) tabulated a total of 11 closed branches compared to 164 identified operating campuses (Becker, 2009). These figures do not include an initial wave of U.S. institutions that established, then terminated, programmatic partnerships with Japanese universities in the 1980s (cf. Chambers & Cummings, 1990; Croom, 2010). Since then, the Cross-Border Education Research Team (C-BERT, 2014) at the State University of New York at Albany has identified more closures, a total of 26 out of 230 identified branch campuses. Despite the small proportion of closed branches compared to those still in operation, commentators have regularly called into question the inherent sustainability of this model of educational provision.

Critics have compared cross-border education provision to academic capitalism, speculating that the benefits are accrued solely to those institutions that are able to behave according to classic market principles, foregoing the public good nature of education (Naidoo, 2007). Given the historical dominance of a north–south model, wherein the home institution from a developed nation establishes a campus in a developing nation, observers have pointed to a replication of neocolonial international relations vis-à-vis academic imperialism, anticipating reduced host country authority and an increase of inequitable access, within both regions and nations (Becker, 2009). Although some wonder if access has not gone far enough, others wonder if IBCs provide too much access with little provisions for quality assurance. Krieger (2008) has doubted the successful provision of high-quality education in environments with poorly prepared students, a limited pool of committed faculty, and truncated academic freedom. We suggest that IBCs are different from other types of cross-border higher education and are better understood when evaluated similarly to an independent campus.

Institutional Effectiveness.   When understood as a type of campus, IBC effectiveness can be evaluated through common metrics like graduation rates, financial sustainability, and organizational capacity. Similarly, by looking at shuttered doors, we can shed some light onto what students, campuses, or governments deem ineffective. Inasmuch as the international branch campus model parallels certain elements of private higher education, these campuses are also likely to close when the form or the function of the institution is no longer viable, as determined by the HEI or the nation state. Closures appear to be related to both campus and government behavior. Ongoing research through C-BERT suggests that an IBC may close due to (a) poor fiscal health caused by low enrollments, high costs, or a combination of both; (b) active government regulation, such as the implementation of quality assurance regimes; or (c) diminished host country support, such as the termination or reversal of previously available financial incentives, legal provisions for privatization, or lack of legitimacy. In other words, IBCs can only be effective as capacity builders when they are organizationally sustainable: Students chose to enroll, administrators manage appropriately, and campus activities fall within the parameters of what is acceptable by the host country laws and regulations.

Community Engagement.   Another substantive type of evaluation can be framed through the civic mission of the branch campus. Similar to institutional effectiveness, the field has developed a broad and deep understanding of the role of community service, often cited next to teaching and research as the core missions of higher education. Many models already exist for assessing civic engagement, one of which is the Carnegie elective community engagement classification framework (Driscoll, 2009). This framework helps campuses to identify and document their connections to their local communities through curricula, faculty hiring processes, community outreach, and partnerships, among other indicators. Although originated in the United States, the Carnegie framework and others like it could be adapted to global environments, providing a mechanism to evaluate IBCs in light of their local constituencies.

Conclusion

As globalization and privatization continue to expand, more campuses and national governments reach across borders to find solutions for their educational needs. Cross-border higher education provides an opportunity to consider how these global trends interact with local forces. As highlighted in this chapter, this rapidly developing subsector of the higher education landscape has demonstrated potential for innovation in delivery and national capacity building, leveraging the resources of existing campuses instead of building infrastructure from scratch. We also highlight numerous inequities in access and quality. Our research indicates that cross-border activities tend to be most successful when administrators and practitioners acknowledge and address the different needs of multiple stakeholders, designing and implementing their initiatives to build capacity. Locally engaged CBHE offers educational activities that are locally relevant and determined by local government and community goals and requirements. These integrated efforts are likely to be the ones that stand the test of time.

References

Alderman, G. (2001). The globalization of higher education: Some observations regarding the free market and the national interest. *Higher Education in Europe, 26*(1), 47–52.

Altbach, P. G., Reisberg, L., & Rumbley, L. (2009). *Trends in global higher education: Tracking an academic revolution.* Paris, France: United States Educational, Scientific and Cultural Organisation.

Auriol, L., Misu, M., & Freeman, R. A. (2013). *Careers of doctorate holders: Analysis of labour market and mobility indicators* (OECD Science, Technology and Industry Working Papers No. 2013/04). Paris, France: Organisation for Economic Co-operation and Development.

Becker, R. (2009). *International branch campuses: Markets and strategies.* London, UK: Observatory on Borderless Higher Education.

Böhm, A., Davis, D., Meares, D., & Pearce, D. (2002). *Global student mobility 2025: Forecasts of the global demand for international higher education.* Sydney, Australia: IDP Education.

Carnevale, A. P., & Rose, S. J. (2012). The convergence of postsecondary education and the labor market. In J. E. Lane & D. B. Johnstone (Eds.), *Colleges and universities as* economic drivers: Measuring higher education's role in economic development (pp. 163–190). Albany: State University of New York Press.

Chambers, G. S., & Cummings, W. K. (1990). Profiting from education: Japan–United States international education ventures in the 1980s. New York, NY: Institute for International Studies.

Coleman, D. (2003). Quality assurance in transnational education. Journal of Studies in International Education, 7(4), 354–378.

Croom, P. (2010). Motivations and aspirations for international branch campuses. In D. W. Chapman & R. Sakamoto (Eds.), Cross border collaborations in higher education: Partnerships beyond the classroom (pp. 45–66). New York, NY: Routledge.

Cross-Border Education Research Team (C-BERT). (2014). Branch campus listing. Retrieved from http://www.globalhighered.org/branchcampuses.php

Daniel, J., Kanwar, A., & Uvalic-Trumbic, S. (2005, April 1). Who's afraid of cross-border higher education? A developing world perspective. Paper presented at the meeting of the International Network of Quality Assurance Agencies in Higher Education, Wellington, New Zealand. Retrieved from http://www.col.org/resources/speeches/2005presentations/Pages/2005-04-01.aspx

Dewey, P., & Duff, S. (2009). Reason before passion: Faculty views on internationalization in higher education. Higher Education, 58(4), 491–504.

Driscoll, A. (2009). Carnegie's new community engagement classification: Affirming higher education's role in community. In L. R. Sandmann, C. H. Thornton, & A. J. Jaeger (Eds.), New Directions for Higher Education: No. 147. Institutionalizing community engagement in higher education: The first wave of Carnegie classified institutions (pp. 5–12). San Francisco, CA: Jossey-Bass.

Frank, D. J., & Gabler, J. (2006). Reconstructing the university: Worldwide shifts in academia in the 20th century. Palo Alto, CA: Stanford University Press.

Harding, L. M., & Lammey, R. W. (2011). Operational considerations for opening a branch campus abroad. In J. E. Lane & K. Kinser (Eds.), New Directions for Higher Education: No. 155. Multinational colleges and universities: Leading, governing, and managing international branch campuses (pp. 65–78). San Francisco, CA: Jossey-Bass.

Ip, C. (2006). Quality assurance for transnational education: A host perspective. In J. Baird (Ed.), Quality audit and assurance for transnational higher education (pp. 21–31). Melbourne, Australia: Australian Universities Quality Agency.

Kanu, Y. (2007). Tradition and educational reconstruction in Africa in postcolonial and global times: The case for Sierra Leone. African Studies Quarterly, 9(3), 65–84.

Kerr, C. (1963). The uses of the university. Cambridge, MA: Harvard University.

Kinser, K. (2011). Multi-national quality assurance. In J. E. Lane & K. Kinser (Eds.), The multi national university: Leadership, administration, and governance of international branch campuses (pp. 53–64). San Francisco, CA: Jossey-Bass.

Kinser, K., & Lane, J. E. (2010). Deciphering "Educational Hubs" strategies: Rhetoric or reality. International Higher Education, 59, 18–19. Retrieved from http://www.academia.edu/1820761/Deciphering_Educational_Hubs_Strategies_Rhetoric_and_Reality

Kinser, K., & Lane, J. E. (2013). Being or building: Branch campuses and cross-border higher education capacity development. IIE Networker, Spring, 43–44.

Knight, J. (2003). GATS, trade and higher education—Perspective 2003—Where are we? London, UK: Observatory on Borderless Higher Education.

Knight, J. (2004). Internationalization remodeled: Definition, approaches, and rationales. Journal of Studies in International Education, 8(1), 5–31.

Knight, J. (2006a). Higher education crossing borders: A guide to the implications of the General Agreement on Trade in Services (GATS) for cross-border education. Paris, France: United Nations Educational, Scientific and Cultural Organization.

Knight, J. (2006b). Crossborder education: An analytical framework for program and provider mobility. Higher education: Handbook of theory and research (Vol. 21, pp. 345–395). Dordrecht, the Netherlands: Springer.

Knight, J. (2011). Education hubs: A fad, a brand, an innovation? *Journal for Studies in International Education*, 15(3), 221–240.

Krieger, Z. (2008). Academic building boom transforms the Persian Gulf. *Education Digest*, 74(1), 4–10.

Lane, J. E. (2010). Joint ventures in cross-border higher education: International branch campuses in Malaysia. In R. Sakamoto & D. W. Chapman (Eds.), *Cross-border collaborations in higher education: Partnerships beyond the classroom* (pp. 67–90). New York, NY: Routledge.

Lane, J. E. (2011). Global expansion of international branch campuses: Managerial and leadership challenges. In J. E. Lane & K. Kinser (Eds.), *New Directions for Higher Education: No. 155. Multinational colleges and universities: Leading, governing, and managing international branch campuses* (pp. 5–17). San Francisco, CA: Jossey-Bass.

Lane, J. E. (2012). Higher education and economic competitiveness. In J. E. Lane & D. B. Johnstone (Eds.), *Colleges and universities as economic drivers: Measuring higher education's role in economic development* (pp. 1–30). Albany: State University of New York Press.

Lane, J. E., & Kinser, K. (2011). Reconsidering privatization in cross-border engagements: The sometimes public nature of private activity. *Higher Education Policy*, 24, 255–273.

Lane, J. E., Kinser, K., & Knox, D. (2012). Regulating cross-border higher education: A case study of the United States. *Higher Education Policy*, 26, 147–172.

Lane, J. E., & Owens, T. L. (2012). The international dimensions of economic development. In J. E. Lane & D. B. Johnstone (Eds.), *Universities and colleges as economic drivers: Measuring and building success* (pp. 205–238). Albany: State University of New York Press.

Levy, D. (2006). The unanticipated explosion: Private higher education's global surge. *Comparative Education Review*, 50(2), 217–240.

Lim, F. C. B. (2009). Education hub at a crossroads: The development of quality assurance as a competitive tool for Singapore's private tertiary education. *Quality Assurance in Education*, 17(1), 79–94.

Lohani, B. N. (2013, May 11). How to build the knowledge economy in the ASEAN. *University World News*. Retrieved from http://www.universityworldnews.com/article.php?story=20130510140627423

McBurnie, G., & Ziguras, C. (2007). *Transnational education: Issues and trends in offshore higher education*. New York, NY: Routledge.

McDermott, D. J. (2014, February 7). Leading the way on regional integration of HE in Asia? *University World News*. Retrieved from http://www.universityworldnews.com/article.php?story=2014020516182133

Naidoo, R. (2007). *Higher education as a global commodity: The perils and promises for developing countries*. London, UK: Observatory on Borderless Education.

National Science Board. (2010). *Science and engineering indicators 2010*. Washington, DC: National Science Foundation.

Organisation for Economic Co-operation and Development (OECD). (2013). *Education at a glance 2013: OECD indicators*. Paris, France: Author.

Picard, E., Bernardino, F., & Ehigiator, K. (2009). Global citizenship for all: Low minority participation in study abroad—Seeking strategies for success. In R. Lewis (Ed.), *The handbook of practice and research in study abroad: Higher education and the quest for global citizenship* (pp. 321–345). New York, NY: Routledge.

Rizvi, F., & Lingard, B. (2010). *Globalizing education policy*. New York, NY: Routledge.

Stella, A. (2006). Quality assurance of cross-border higher education. *Quality in Higher Education*, 12(3), 257–276.

United Nations Educational, Scientific and Cultural Organization (UNESCO). (1997). *Recommendation concerning the status of higher education teaching personnel.* Paris, France: Author.
van der Wende, M. C. (2003). Globalization and access to higher education. *Journal of Studies in International Education, 7*(2), 193–206.
Wildavsky, B. (2010). *The great brain race: How global universities are reshaping the world.* Princeton, NJ: Princeton University Press.

TAYA L. OWENS currently serves the State University of New York system office of academic affairs with system-wide program implementation and research.

JASON E. LANE is vice provost for academic affairs and senior associate vice chancellor at State University of New York, as well as associate professor and codirector of the Cross-Border Education Research Team (C-BERT) at the State University of New York at Albany.

This chapter focuses on the development of education hubs, a recent phenomenon in international higher education. Three models of hubs are examined in relation to the forces, risks, and opportunities of globalization and how local and international collaborations are essential for both global competitiveness and sustainability.

International Education Hubs: Collaboration for Competitiveness and Sustainability

Jane Knight

During the past three decades, international higher education has mushroomed and dramatically changed in response to the forces and opportunities of globalization. Although lively debate continues as to whether higher education internationalization is a "response" or an "agent" of globalization, few doubt that there has been an increased flow of ideas, people, technology, goods, values, capital, services, and knowledge around the world. As a result, interdependence and interconnectivity among countries have intensified. Higher education has played a pivotal role in contributing to the flow of people, knowledge, values, and economy, and has significantly impacted the changing international engagement landscape (Altbach, 2013).

Globalization is a rather subjective term as it is interpreted in a myriad of ways according to the norms, context, and perspectives of the policymaker, scholar, or general public. The impact of globalization has been a hot topic in popular and scholarly discourse for many years, with its positive benefits, negative impacts, and unintended consequences being analyzed and contested. Although globalization is recognized as a "new normal," the debate is appropriately moving into analyzing how regions, countries, communities, and sectors can mediate the realities of globalization to maximize potential benefits and mitigate potential risks. The purpose of this chapter is to examine international education hubs—one of the newest developments in the international landscape of higher education—and to explore how hubs are both actors and reactors to the multiple dimensions and manifestations of globalization.

New Directions for Higher Education, no. 168, Winter 2014 © 2014 Wiley Periodicals, Inc.
Published online in Wiley Online Library (wileyonlinelibrary.com) • DOI: 10.1002/he.20115

The international dimension of higher education has existed for centuries through the exchange of scholars and knowledge around the world. The fact that "universe" is the root concept for the term "university" is clear evidence of its internationality. But the priorities and strategies of international higher education have twisted and turned over the years in response to the globalized environment in which it operates. Different rationales and opportunities have driven an unprecedented increase in international education (Altbach, Reisberg, & Rumbley, 2009; Knight, 2008).

The number of students moving around the world in search of academic programs, exchanges, and qualifications has increased exponentially in the past 50 years. For example, international students in foreign countries expanded from 238,000 in the 1960s (Chen & Barnett, 2000) to 4.1 million in 2010 (Organisation for Economic Co-operation and Development, 2012), and it is estimated that 7.8 million students will be enrolled in tertiary education in foreign countries by 2025 (Böhm, Davis, Meares, & Pearce, 2002). But it is not only people who are moving across borders—so are education programs, providers, projects, and policies. The number of twinning programs, joint/double degree programs, and exchange programs has multiplied 10 times in the past two decades. The development of international branch campuses in foreign countries has increased from 24 in 2002 to over 230 in 2011 (Lawton & Katsomitrous, 2012). Binational universities are a new development in the landscape of higher education and demonstrate the close bilateral links between the higher education sectors of two countries in the establishment of a new joint institution (Knight, 2013).

International education hubs are the latest development in this landscape. They represent a wider and more strategic configuration of actors and activities, building on and including many of the recent developments in cross-border higher education detailed in Chapter 6 of this volume. An education hub may be described as a critical mass of education and knowledge actors aiming to exert greater influence in the new education marketplace and to strengthen relations between local and international counterparts. The concept of an education hub is driven by many factors, including a country's motivation to position itself as a reputed center for higher education and research. Local, regional, and international students, institutions, knowledge industries, government agencies, and research and development centers are integral to the establishment and operation of education hubs (Knight, 2011). Collaboration among the different actors is key to making the hub locally sustainable and globally competitive. Scholars and policymakers note that education hubs can be effective tools for increasing a country's attractiveness and influence; modernizing higher education policies and practices while increasing access to education; recruiting, training, and retaining a skilled work force; furthering economic development; shifting to a knowledge- and service-based economy; and building strategic and influential alliances (Cheng, Cheung, & Yeun, 2011; Mok, 2008).

A Working Definition of Education Hubs

The proposed definition outlined in this section is based on Knight's (2011) analysis of existing education hub countries and the current diversity of cross-border activities. Working on the assumption that the number and types of education hubs will increase over time, the proposed working definition is generic enough to apply to different levels of education hubs (i.e., at the zone or city level) even though this chapter only focuses on country-level hubs. An education hub is "a planned effort to build a critical mass of local and international actors strategically engaged in education, training, knowledge production and innovation initiatives" (Knight, 2011, p. 227). This definition attempts to capture the fundamental elements of an education hub regardless of the primary actors or its geographic location (see Knight, 2011, for a fuller discussion of the definition). To fully understand the meaning and dimensions of this working definition, it is helpful to examine each of the five major concepts within it.

First, the concept of "planned effort" indicates that a hub is an intentional or deliberate project that would normally involve a strategy, a policy framework, and an investment. In other words, a hub is more than a coincidental interaction or colocation of actors working in the education and knowledge sectors. The notion of being planned helps to decrease the chances that an education hub is merely a fad or branding exercise. Second, the notion of "critical mass" suggests that there is more than one actor and set of activities involved. This means that a single-branch campus, franchise program, or science and technology park does not constitute a hub. The concept of critical mass intentionally goes beyond a random collection of cross-border activities as it denotes that there is a key combination of actors to ensure that the impact of the whole (the hub) is greater than the sum of its parts.

Third, the inclusion of "local and international actors" indicates that an education hub involves both domestic and foreign players. They may include local, regional, and international actors, such as scholars, institutions, companies, organizations, research centers, and knowledge industries. The term "actor" is used in an inclusive manner to cover providers, producers, and users of the hub's education offerings, training, knowledge services, and products. The diversity of actors will vary from hub to hub depending on the rationales and functions of the hub; thus, types of actors are intentionally not specified in the definition. Fourth, the idea of "strategically engaged" is central to the definition as it emphasizes that there is a deliberate sense of interaction or relationship among the actors. Although the nature of the engagement will differ from hub to hub, a fundamental principle is that there is added value when the actors are connected, collaborating, or sharing common facilities and resources. This fact does not deny that there will be competition among actors who offer similar services or products, but the benefits of being part of a strategic and interactive initiative appear to outweigh the challenges. The nature and number of interactions are unlimited given the diversity of local and international actors and users. Fifth, "education, training, knowledge production and innovation initiatives" depict the broad categories of activities and outputs of hubs. There is a wide selection of initiatives or services that are available depending on the type of hub, priorities of the individual actors, and the sponsor's strategic plan.

Additionally, an education hub has not been defined in physical or spatial terms (such as a designated area) as this may be too limiting. Rather, the central concept is one of a strategically connected and engaged set of local and international actors undertaking cross-border education activities to achieve their individual objectives as well as the collective goals and outcomes of the sponsoring body, whether it is a city, zone, or country.

A Typology of Education Hubs: Student, Talent, and Knowledge/Innovation

As indicated earlier, different rationales, actors, and activities characterize education hubs. Some countries see hubs as a means to build a critical mass of international students and providers to generate income, as well as to modernize and internationalize their domestic higher education systems. Others seek to be a hub in order to train foreign and local students and employees to be part of a skilled labor force. Other countries focus on building a vibrant research, knowledge, and innovation sector that will lead their nations into the knowledge economy.

A suggested typology of three categories of education hubs (Student, Talent, and Knowledge/Innovation) captures the differences among hub approaches and allows for a more nuanced understanding and exploration of education hubs (Knight, 2011). This typology is based on the rationales driving hub development, rather than on the location or level of hubs.

The Student hub focuses on the education and training of local, expatriate, and international students. In addition to recruiting students, it also focuses on attracting foreign higher education institutions (HEIs) to offer franchised and twinning programs or establish branch campuses in order to increase access for all types of students. The primary objectives for Student hubs are: (a) to provide increased access to higher education for local students; (b) to generate revenue from international student fees; (c) to build capacity of local HEIs; (d) to internationalize the domestic higher education system; and (e) to enhance profile, branding, and ranking of HEIs and countries.

In this scenario, both local HEIs and foreign providers recruit local and international students to their programs and campuses. A national recruitment strategy and related policies are generally in place to successfully grow a Student education hub. Such a plan may include an overall numerical target of foreign students, cross-border programs, or international branch campuses (IBCs) in order to gain a regional or global reputation as an attractive place to get a quality education. A Student hub often gives priority to foreign student enrollment even though there is an interest in providing wider access for local students. Foreign students are recruited to complete their studies in the host country and then return home or move to a third country. Generally, they are not encouraged or provided incentives to stay in the host country. A Student hub may aim to attract students from all parts of the world, but in many cases the majority of students come from neighboring countries in the region.

The Talent hub focuses on student education and training, but differs from the Student hub given that the overarching goal is human resource development for a skilled work force. International students are encouraged to remain in the host country for employment purposes, and retention of these students (and workers) is central to the Talent hub. International HEIs, as well as private training/education companies, are encouraged to offer academic programs and professional development opportunities aimed at international, expatriate, and national students as well as local employees for human resource development. The driving objectives are: (a) to expand the talent pool of skilled workers, (b) to build a service- or knowledge-based economy, (c) to increase economic competiveness and influence in the region and beyond, and (d) to strengthen the quality and relevance of labor. The education/training institutions and providers are often, but not necessarily, colocated to facilitate the use of shared facilities and promote collaboration among them and with industry. In order to develop a critical mass, there may be more than one colocation site in a country.

The Knowledge/Innovation hub broadens its mandate beyond education and training to include the production and distribution of knowledge and innovation. Foreign actors include universities, research institutes, and companies with major research and development activities. All these actors are attracted through favorable business incentives to establish a base in the country and to collaborate with local partners in developing applied research, knowledge, and innovation. The primary objectives are: (a) to build a knowledge- and innovation-based economy, (b) to attract foreign direct investment, (c) to build capacity of local research and development centers, (d) to increase competitiveness, and (e) to enhance attractiveness and influence as a political actor. Collaboration among the key players—foreign and local education institutions, industries, research centers, and companies—is a key factor in building a Knowledge/Innovation hub and in providing added value for the major actors.

Highlights of Six International Education Hubs

As of 2014, there are six international country-level education hubs in different stages of implementation. They are located in three different regions of the world—the Middle East, South East Asia, and Africa—and include Qatar, the United Arab Emirates, Hong Kong, Malaysia, Singapore, and

Botswana. These six countries/jurisdictions are very different but all are relatively small and committed to moving their economies from dependence on national resources or manufacturing to one based on knowledge and service industries. Other countries, such as South Korea, Sri Lanka, and Mauritius, are currently trying to position themselves as hubs. Some countries' intentions are more of a branding campaign to attract international students or education providers, whereas others are moving forward with strategic plans and significant investments.

The term "education hub" is a subjective and self-ascribed label. There is no exclusive set of indicators or official body that determines whether a country meets stated requirements to be called an education hub. Therefore, as the popularity and "branding value" of the concept increases, so does the number of countries that seek to be an education hub.

Also important to note is that "one size does not fit all" when it comes to international education hubs. Although there may be some similarity in terms of driving rationales to become an education hub, the approaches, plans, and strategies differ according to the priorities and local context of each country. Table 7.1 summarizes several major features of each hub country and is based on in-depth case studies by experts in each country (see Knight, 2014a). The start-up date for each of the six hubs shows that both Qatar and Singapore had the vision of becoming a hub almost two decades ago, whereas Botswana and Hong Kong have been established more recently. The slower rate of progress for the newer hub countries may be linked to the world economic crisis of 2008/2009, which curtailed investments and plans. Most interesting is the comparison of what type of hub each country is now and what it aspires to be.

Singapore is one of the most developed and successful hubs. It has moved over the past 15 years from its "Global Schoolhouse" project, which concentrated on recruiting foreign students and prestigious universities, to its current strategy, which emphasizes investing in major research initiatives and facilities to establish sustainable international research partnerships (Sidhu, Ho, & Yeoh, 2014). Its current emphasis is squarely on research, knowledge production, and innovation. Based on the previously described typology, Singapore can be categorized as a Knowledge/Innovation education hub.

Qatar has taken another approach by developing itself as a Student/Talent education hub with aspirations of being a Knowledge/Innovation education hub. Its centerpiece is "Education City," which houses 10 prestigious universities from the United States and United Kingdom, all of which have been invited and generously supported by the Qatar Foundation that oversees the strategy and development of the country hub plans. A Science and Technology Park is another core element and was established in a free zone. Developing international research partnerships, building research facilities, training researchers, and developing a research

Table 7.1. Features of Six International Education Hubs

	Qatar	UAE	HK	Malaysia	Singapore	Botswana
Start-Up Date	1995	2003	2008	2007	1998	2008
Progress	High	High	Low	Mod-High	High	Low
Features	Education City with 10 IBCs Science and Tech Park in free zone Major investment in research facilities, projects, HRD	Multiple free zones that house more than 37 IBCs Emphasis on education and training for expats living in UAE Recruit international students	Focus on recruiting "nonlocal students" primarily from Mainland China New scholarships and immigration policies in place	Strategy to recruit foreign students 7 IBCs around the country New free zone with HEIs and schools	Major investment in facilities, programs, HRD for international research partnership 18 IBCs Foreign students constitute 10% of all enrollments	Novel strategy to have education hub provide skilled labor to five industrial hubs Focus on attracting more foreign students and branch campuses
Current Hub Type	Talent/Student	Student/Talent	Student	Student	Knowledge	Student
Aspiration	Talent/Knowledge	Talent/Knowledge	Talent	Talent/Knowledge	Knowledge	Student/Talent

Note: Adapted from Knight (2014a).

culture in the country, as well as providing major research grant programs, is the third strand to the Qatar approach (Ibnouf, Dou, & Knight, 2014).

The United Arab Emirates (UAE), a neighbor of Qatar, can be labeled as a Student/Talent education hub and has used a very different model. Four of the seven emirates have recruited international branch campuses to provide increased access for expatriate and domestic students. The Knowledge Village in Dubai and the Dubai International Academic City are the best known free zones and together host about 25 of the 37 IBCs in UAE. A free zone can be described as a commercial approach and offers tax and financial incentives to attract IBCs. Using an investment approach, Abu Dhabi, the wealthiest emirate, has invited and generously supported elite universities from the United States and France and has invested in research partnerships with foreign universities to develop centers of excellence, such as Masdar City. There is no overall country-level strategy for developing UAE as an education hub. This has led to the diversity of approaches, which seem to have been successfully used to date (Fox & Al Shamisi, 2014).

Malaysia is a country with a long history of international education. It has developed a comprehensive but diversified approach to positioning itself as a Student education hub with long-term aspirations of being a Knowledge education hub. Over the past decade, seven IBCs have been established throughout the country, and there are more in the pipeline for approval. Malaysia has doubled its number of international students using its attractiveness to Muslim students as a key feature. An ambitious new free zone abutting Singapore, Iskandar is under development and is already home to several branch campuses of major international universities. Other policies and programs have been established that aim to increase Malaysia's attractiveness and competitiveness as an education hub. Its efforts to date have focused on education and training rather than on research (Aziz & Abdullah, 2014).

Hong Kong's intentions and policy statements about being positioned as an education hub have been clear, but the plans to move forward are less visible (Mok & Bodycott, 2014). Troubled by the economic downturn in 2008, Hong Kong's efforts have focused on offering scholarships and recruiting more "nonlocal students"—a term used to describe students from the region and Mainland China who officially cannot be classified as foreign or international students. Given the priority to recruit students, it sees itself as a Student education hub, and as immigration policies change and more students stay and work in Hong Kong, it aspires to be more of a Talent education hub.

Botswana has taken a rather innovative approach to planning its development as a Talent education hub. To broaden its economic base, Botswana has identified and prioritized five different industrial hub sectors and areas for investment. Each one requires competent and trained professionals, and the country envisions the role of the education hub as serving to educate, train, and supply the required labor. Although Botswana has taken steps to attract more foreign students and international branch campuses, progress has been moderated by financial challenges. The extensive consultation and planning process has provided a firm foundation to work toward being a Talent education hub, but finding resources to implement the plan is taking longer than the government anticipated (John, Wilmoth, & Mokopakgosi, 2014).

Education Hub Rationales in the Context of Globalization

The above analysis reveals that there are myriad rationales driving a country to establish itself as an education hub. The rationales can be seen as catalysts propelling a country to consider how to respond to the forces, opportunities, and impacts of globalization, and to determine their role and relationships in the region and beyond.

The diversity of rationales driving international higher education in general and education hubs in particular can be sorted into five major groups or categories. The categories emerged from a careful analysis of the six hub countries, and thus reflect the realities of their local, regional, and international contexts (see Knight, 2014a, for a fuller discussion). The groups overlap and interplay, reflecting both the complexities and challenges of mediating the forces and effects of globalization. The following section provides elaboration on the five groups of rationales, and Table 7.2 shows the importance of the rationales as determined from a recent study on education hubs (Knight, 2014b).

Table 7.2. Level of Importance of Rationales

Rationales	Overall Rank
Economic	1
Diversify economy	
Income generation	
Attract investment	
Education and Training	2
Quality of HE system	
Access for students	
Skill training	
Skilled Work Force	3
Attract foreign talent	
Retain local/foreign workers	
Prepare skilled work force	
Status	4
Recognition in region/world	
Improve competitiveness	
Geopolitical influence	
Research	5
Knowledge production	
Innovation application	

Note: Adapted from Knight (2014b).

Economic reasons constitute the first category of rationales, and are linked to all three types of education hubs. Economic reasons are dominant and take many forms. For instance, strengthening the education industry (a term often used in hub discussions) is the principal economic rationale, whereas attracting foreign investment is a second rationale. Support for economic diversification by building a more pervasive knowledge and service economy is a common and influential third economic motivation. These rationales are often linked to the neoliberal market orientation of globalization and the move toward a knowledge-based economy. They provide evidence of commercialization for critics who believe that higher education has been both commodified and commercialized and is being used for economic purposes. On the other hand, universities, educational organizations, and Ministries of Education are facing the reality of having to look for alternative sources of funding and investment in education. This has led to the rise of public–private partnerships that are both national and international in scope. Education hubs bring together a variety of local and international players, private and public partnerships, and actors who collaborate and compete in a strategic approach to international higher education.

The second category consists of education and training reasons and is linked to Student and Talent education hubs. It is necessary to use the term "education and training reasons" rather than "academic rationales" because education hubs differentiate between academic activities (such as teaching and training) and projects related to research and knowledge production. Three core motives in this category include: (a) improving access to learning opportunities for local, expatriate, and international students; (b) aligning education and training with industry needs; and (c) enhancing the overall quality of higher education in the host country. These motivations demonstrate the interconnectedness and somewhat interdependent nature of the higher education landscape around the world. Countries without the capacity or the political will to meet the growing demand for increased access to tertiary education seek to collaborate with foreign partners to offer additional academic programs through joint efforts such as international branch campuses, binational universities, and twinning or franchise programs. Furthermore, the internationalization of quality assurance is evidence of academic policy mobility, which can help build capacity and/or lead to standardization—a threat often associated with globalization. Key to international academic collaboration is ensuring respect for local culture, norms, practices, and priorities; "copy and paste" is not an appropriate or useful approach to policy or program mobility.

Knowledge generation and innovation is the third category of rationales and is directly tied to the Knowledge/Innovation type of education hub. It focuses on strengthening research culture, capacity, and output, as well as providing support for applied research. As previously discussed, globalization is often linked with the shift to a knowledge economy and society. In such a context, higher education has a major role to play given that one of academia's key mandates is research and knowledge production, and, more recently, application of knowledge through innovation. The growth in bilateral and multilateral research networks and projects increases the potential to address international issues such as pandemics, crimes, climate concerns, environmental issues, and human rights by combining strengths and expertise of scientists, scholars, and experts from across the globe. A prerequisite for education hubs to advance knowledge/innovation thus represents respect for diversity of expertise, national needs and priorities, mutuality of benefits, and intellectual property right protection. These are critical factors in mediating the potential negative impact of the power imbalances often associated with globalization.

The fourth category emphasizes human resource development, which is fundamental to the Talent education hub. The need for trained, skilled workers in the transformation to a knowledge- and service-based economy is a leading rationale. A second rationale is the need to prevent "brain drain" by retaining local and foreign talent in the country. The mobility of talent and labor across the world is directly linked to the flow of people cited in the description of globalization at the beginning of this chapter. A consequence related to this rationale is that the attraction and retention of skilled labor means "brain gain" for some countries and potential brain drain for others. To ward off criticisms of brain drain, the term "brain circulation" has gained currency in popular and scholarly discourse (Lee & Kim, 2010). Although there is an inherent truth to the circulation of talent, the term is often used to "whitewash" or neutralize the negative connotations linked with brain drain. Another way to conceptualize talent mobility is the term "brain chain," where there is movement from country to country; however, in the end, those at the bottom of the chain are net losers and this represents a negative impact of globalization and competition for human resources, one that needs to be addressed. Also worth noting is that the human resource development rationale applies to the development and retention of local citizens and, in some cases, long-term expatriates. As the shift to service-centered and knowledge-based industries occurs, the professional development and training of the local workforce is critical, and this is another factor driving education Talent hubs.

The fifth category of rationales is harder to label because it involves using the education hub for status, soft power, or geopolitical influence. This rationale relates to all three types of education hubs. The primary motives included in this category are: (a) to promote or brand the country (or jurisdiction) as a regional/global center of excellence, (b) to use education to increase attractiveness or competitiveness and status within the region and beyond, and (c) to create international partnerships for education and research. It is this set of rationales that addresses the competitiveness agenda and the use of higher education to gain recognition and geopolitical influence. Depending on the type of hub, competitiveness can relate to a variety of aspects, such as: (a) attracting top-ranked elite HEIs for collaboration or as symbols of power, (b) attracting foreign investment for science and technology parks and research projects, (c) increased profile as a preferred education destination as well as a source of revenue gained from direct and indirect income streams related to foreign students, (d) leadership and/or membership in prestigious academic networks, (e) attracting world-renowned scientists for research initiatives, and (f) accumulation of international patents for inventions or applications. This list reflects the current obsession of many countries to be highly ranked (as Ellen Hazelkorn explains in Chapter 2) and associated with prestigious partners in order to maximize their brand and profile as a center of higher education excellence or a powerful marketplace of education activities. This speaks to status-building motives for becoming an education hub, not to capacity building. Hubs built purely for status, branding, and profile are unlikely to be sustainable as the investments needed for long-term hub development are not forthcoming given the short term, more public relations intentions and approach to building an education hub.

Conclusions: The Importance of Collaboration Among Policy Sectors

A variety of policy sectors and key actors are involved in the planning, development, and operation of different education hubs. These may include education, trade and export, science/technology, labor, foreign affairs, immigration, economic development, industry, and culture, among others. For example, the key policy sectors for the Talent hub would likely include immigration, labor, and industry. But for a Knowledge/Innovation hub, science and technology, economic development, and trade are the major players. This demonstrates that although education may be considered a vital policy sector for planning and overseeing an education hub, it does not always take the lead, and must work in conjunction with other influential policy areas. But, collaboration among different policy sectors and their lead actors is not always easy or straightforward, as different and competing agendas are at play. Allocating resources and assuring political will for cross-sector initiatives require careful negotiation and balancing of diverse interests. Unless the actors in various policy sectors look for the greater common good for their countries and establish agreements and compromises, their efforts to develop and sustain education hubs in order to optimize local needs and priorities are in jeopardy.

   This chapter has focused on the key features, rationales, and policy sectors involved in three different models of education hubs. It examines how collaboration among diverse domestic policy sectors such as education, labor, industry, trade, and immigration is essential in the strategic planning and development of the hub. Furthermore, cooperation among the diversity of local and international actors—higher education institutions and providers, students, research and development centers, and knowledge industries—is critical to ensure that the education hub is competitive and sustainable. In short, collaboration and cooperation among local policy sectors and between domestic and international actors are fundamental strategies in mediating the forces and opportunities of globalization for countries that are actively engaged and committed to becoming education hubs.

References

Altbach, P. G. (2013). *The international imperative in higher education.* Rotterdam, the Netherlands: Sense.

Altbach, P. G., Reisberg, L., & Rumbley, L. (2009). *Trends in global higher education: Tracking an academic revolution.* Chestnut Hill, MA: Center for International Higher Education, Boston College.

Aziz, M. I. A., & Abdullah, D. (2014). Malaysia: Becoming an education hub to serve national development. In J. Knight (Ed.), *International education hubs: Student, talent, knowledge/innovation models* (pp. 101–120). Dordrecht, the Netherlands: Springer.

Böhm, A., Davis, D., Meares, D., & Pearce, D. (2002). *The global student mobility 2025 report: Forecasts of the global demand for international education.* Sydney, Australia: IDP Education.

Chen, T., & Barnett, G. (2000). Research on international student flows from a macro perspective: A network analysis of 1985, 1989 and 1995. *Higher Education, 39,* 435–453.

Cheng, Y. C., Cheung, A. C. K., & Yeun, T. W. W. (2011). Development of a regional education hub: The case of Hong Kong. *International Journal of Educational Management, 25*(5), 474–493.

Fox, W. H., & Al Shamisi, S. (2014). United Arab Emirates' education hub: A decade of development. In J. Knight (Ed.), *International education hubs: Student, talent, knowledge/innovation models* (pp. 63–80). Dordrecht, the Netherlands: Springer.

Ibnouf, A., Dou, L., & Knight, J. (2014). The evolution of Qatar as an education hub: Moving to a knowledge-based economy. In J. Knight (Ed.), *International education hubs: Student, talent, knowledge/innovation models* (pp. 43–62). Dordrecht, the Netherlands: Springer.

John, B. P., Wilmoth, J. D., & Mokopakgosi, B. (2014). Botswana country hub: Africa's first education hub. In J. Knight (Ed.), *International education hubs: Student, talent, knowledge/innovation models* (pp. 145–164). Dordrecht, the Netherlands: Springer.

Knight, J. (2008). *Higher education in turmoil: The changing world of internationalization.* Rotterdam, the Netherlands: Sense.

Knight, J. (2011). Education hubs: A fad, a brand or an innovation? *Journal for Studies in International Education, 15*(3), 221–240.

Knight, J. (2013). The changing landscape of higher education internationalization—For better or worse? *Perspectives: Policy and Practice in Higher Education, 17*(2), 84–90.

Knight J. (2014a). (Ed.). *International education hubs: Student, talent, knowledge/innovation models.* Dordrecht, the Netherlands: Springer.

Knight J. (2014b). Understanding education hubs within the context of crossborder education. In J. Knight (Ed.), *International education hubs: Student, talent, knowledge/innovation models* (pp. 12–28). Dordrecht, the Netherlands: Springer.

Lawton, W., & Katsomitrous, A. (2012). *International branch campuses: Data and developments.* London, UK: Observatory on Borderless Higher Education.

Lee, J., & Kim, D. (2010). Brain gain or brain circulation? US doctoral recipients returning to South Korea. *Higher Education, 59*(5), 627–643.

Mok, K. H. (2008). Singapore's global education hub ambitions: University governance change and transnational higher education. *International Journal of Education Management, 22*(6), 527–546.

Mok, K. H., & Bodycott, P. (2014). Hong Kong: The quest for regional education hub status. In J. Knight (Ed.), *International education hubs: Student, talent, knowledge/innovation models* (pp. 81–100). Dordrecht, the Netherlands: Springer.

Organisation for Economic Co-operation and Development. (2012). *Education at a glance 2012*. Paris, France: Author.

Sidhu, R., Ho, K.-C., & Yeoh, S. A. (2014). Singapore: Building a knowledge and education hub. In J. Knight (Ed.), *International education hubs: Student, talent, knowledge/innovation models* (pp. 131–144). Dordrecht, the Netherlands: Springer.

JANE KNIGHT is affiliated with the Ontario Institute for Studies in Education at the University of Toronto.

NEW DIRECTIONS FOR HIGHER EDUCATION • DOI: 10.1002/he

8

In this final chapter of the volume, the editors synthesize key themes that emerge from the preceding chapters. They also highlight the contributions the authors make through emphasizing critical perspectives and the tension between global and local forces.

A Critical Analysis of Global Competition in Higher Education: Synthesizing Themes

Laura M. Portnoi, Sylvia S. Bagley

The chapters in this volume interrogate key facets of global competition in higher education, raising important social justice concerns. The authors situate their topics within current international scholarship and offer critical analyses that counter the dominant normative approach to studying global competition in higher education. Next, we discuss four themes evident throughout the chapters.

The Changing Higher Education Landscape

The rapidly changing nature of higher education is clear throughout this volume. One of the most fundamental developments is increased internationalization. Although higher education has always been international in nature, heightened internationalization in recent years—evidenced by increasing collaboration between higher education institutions (HEIs) across borders—has significantly impacted the sector (Knight, Chapter 7). Greater internationalization, propelled in part by growing transparency through technological advances, has led to a heightened awareness of other HEIs and their operations, as well as intensified comparisons of status and reputation. In this context, seeking prestige is frequently tied to an HEI's global reach (Owens & Lane, Chapter 6).

In the emergent knowledge economy, governments increasingly view HEIs as central to producing the human capital that drives national economic advancement (Hazelkorn, Chapter 2). Governments and HEIs are emphasizing research to a greater extent—at the expense of teaching and service to local communities (Hazelkorn, Chapter 2; Rhoads, Li, & Ilano, Chapter 3). With the advent of the World Trade Organization's General Agreement on Trades and Services, higher education has become a

NEW DIRECTIONS FOR HIGHER EDUCATION, no. 168, Winter 2014 © 2014 Wiley Periodicals, Inc.
Published online in Wiley Online Library (wileyonlinelibrary.com) • DOI: 10.1002/he.20116

commodity that can be traded, marketed, and branded, as Rhoads et al. contend in Chapter 3. Privatization has also had a profound effect on the higher education sector, and on quality assurance in particular. In Chapter 5, Kinser suggests that the proliferation of private HEIs, especially those that cross borders, has been a driver of the quality assurance regime. Questions about the potential for neocolonialism also arise, especially given the spread of international branch campuses (Owens & Lane, Chapter 6).

Massification and greater demand for entry into higher education are additional hallmarks of the current global higher education landscape. With the aforementioned developments comes a call for greater accountability, especially from external stakeholders given that the neoliberal agenda has resulted in an overall decline in public trust (Kinser, Chapter 5). All of these changes lead to an increasingly hierarchical and competitive environment in the global higher education sector, with undue focus on prestige and status at the expense of more localized and equity-oriented concerns.

The Drive Toward Global Competition

The changing higher education landscape contributes to and is impacted by the drive toward global competition. With increasing accountability and awareness of competitors both within and outside local boundaries, it is not surprising that global higher education rankings have taken on such significance. In Chapter 2, Hazelkorn contends that rankings are often about geopolitical positioning and therefore profoundly influence higher education decision making. Given rankings' emphasis on research productivity, which connects to knowledge production, they have become even more salient in the globally competitive higher education sector (Hazelkorn, Chapter 2; Rhoads et al., Chapter 3). Accordingly, securing a spot on one of the most widely recognized ranking systems—especially through the creation or fostering of world-class HEIs—has become an institutional and national obsession for many.

The focus on rankings and status leads to a competitive environment in which governments and HEIs employ various strategies to improve their stature, such as building world-class universities or increasing their cross-border offerings. Additionally, governments and HEIs increasingly compete for (top) international scholars and students (Owens & Lane, Chapter 6). Competition within the higher education sector is no longer local or even national in nature, but rather has become increasingly global.

Social Justice Considerations

Along with rapid changes in the higher education landscape and an increased drive toward global competition come a host of social justice concerns. One is the threat to the notion of "public good." In Chapter 2, Hazelkorn asks whether HEIs, particularly elite research universities, are becoming self-serving, privatized organizations that lack commitment to their local contexts and constituents. HEIs are considered key to a nation's economic prowess, leading to promotion of top HEIs and a concentration of resources and wealth at elite institutions that typically serve the most affluent populations. Mergers aimed at creating world-class universities add to this consolidation of resources (Välimaa, Aittola, & Ursin, Chapter 4). As selectivity of both faculty and students increases, so does the perceived and actual value of elite institutions (Hazelkorn, Chapter 2), with one ideal HEI model—the elite research university—rising to the top, thus reinforcing existing hierarchies (Rhoads et al., Chapter 3). In Chapter 3, Rhoads et al. contend that the rankings' metrics are proxies for institutional wealth, and pose specific alternatives emphasizing socially conscious concerns.

Meanwhile, Kinser points out in Chapter 5 that standards—like rankings—are normative and reflect a specific, value-laden philosophy about what is important. When examining any given quality assurance mechanism, questions of whose ideals are reflected and whose purposes are served inevitably arise. Another factor is that access to educational opportunities is generally reserved for those with sufficient financial resources; additionally, foreign outposts of elite HEIs may not offer the same quality of service for the students they serve in host countries (Owens & Lane, Chapter 6). Cross-border higher education (CBHE)—including international education hubs—also raises concerns about academic capitalism and neocolonialism stemming from dominant and resource-rich Western influences.

Throughout this volume, the authors raise many provocative questions regarding social justice and global competition within higher education. The overall mission and purpose of higher education as a public good are at the center of these challenging discussions.

Tensions Between Global and Local Forces

A final theme evident throughout this volume is the tension between global and local forces. Although global competition trends are prominent, context is critically important. The Finnish merger case provides an interesting example of how local forces respond to and resist global trends in context-specific ways (Välimaa et al., Chapter 4). Clearly, local traditions and public voice do matter. In Chapter 5, Kinser suggests that local norms and relevance are important for quality assurance, as there is no one-size-fits-all model covering all jurisdictions. For example, he points out that China has constructed its own regulatory system, rejecting dominant Western models. Curricular relevance across local contexts is also important within CBHE (Owens & Lane, Chapter 6). Owens and Lane (Chapter 6) argue for locally relevant offerings; their research shows that arrangements involving input from key players in the host country are most likely to be sustainable. Similarly, in Chapter 7, Jane Knight suggests that in order for international education hubs to be successful, local jurisdictions, national governments, and communities must be able to maximize their potential benefits while mitigating risks. She emphasizes that hubs themselves are actors that choose different models based on the purpose and needs of the local context. Clearly, local priorities do (and should) play a significant role.

Concluding Remarks

Our purpose with this volume of *New Directions for Higher Education* is to offer critical perspectives on global competition in higher education, focusing on the tension between global and local forces. Although the drive toward global competition in the sector is evident, it is not monolithic or static. Context is vitally important and there are no universal measures. Taken together, the chapters in this volume highlight vernacular globalization, or how local forces mediate global trends (Appadurai, 1996). The authors demonstrate the myriad avenues through which local actors may intervene and respond to these developments. They interrogate the potential for social injustice that arises, posing critical questions about the impact of global competition in an increasingly hierarchical higher education environment. By providing an invaluable alternative perspective to the descriptive, normative approach that dominates the scholarship on global competition in higher education, the chapters in this volume open a fresh dialogue in this arena.

Reference

Appadurai, A. (1996). *Modernity at large: Cultural dimensions of globalization*. Minneapolis: University of Minnesota Press.

LAURA M. PORTNOI is an associate professor and assistant department chair in the Advanced Studies in Education and Counseling Department at California State University, Long Beach.

SYLVIA S. BAGLEY is director of Teacher Leadership in the College of Education at the University of Washington.

NEW DIRECTIONS FOR HIGHER EDUCATION • DOI: 10.1002/he

INDEX

NEW DIRECTIONS FOR HIGHER EDUCATION

ORDER FORM SUBSCRIPTION AND SINGLE ISSUES

DISCOUNTED BACK ISSUES:

Use this form to receive 20% off all back issues of *New Directions for Higher Education*.
All single issues priced at **$23.20** (normally $29.00)

TITLE	ISSUE NO.	ISBN

Call 1-800-835-6770 or see mailing instructions below. When calling, mention the promotional code JBNND to receive your discount. For a complete list of issues, please visit www.josseybass.com/go/ndhe

SUBSCRIPTIONS: (1 YEAR, 4 ISSUES)

☐ New Order   ☐ Renewal

U.S.	☐ Individual: $89	☐ Institutional: $335
CANADA/MEXICO	☐ Individual: $89	☐ Institutional: $375
ALL OTHERS	☐ Individual: $113	☐ Institutional: $409

Call 1-800-835-6770 or see mailing and pricing instructions below.
Online subscriptions are available at www.onlinelibrary.wiley.com

ORDER TOTALS:

Issue / Subscription Amount: $ _____

Shipping Amount: $ _____
(for single issues only – subscription prices include shipping)

Total Amount: $ _____

SHIPPING CHARGES:

First Item	$6.00
Each Add'l Item	$2.00

(No sales tax for U.S. subscriptions. Canadian residents, add GST for subscription orders. Individual rate subscriptions must be paid by personal check or credit card. Individual rate subscriptions may not be resold as library copies.)

BILLING & SHIPPING INFORMATION:

☐ **PAYMENT ENCLOSED:** *(U.S. check or money order only. All payments must be in U.S. dollars.)*

☐ **CREDIT CARD:** ☐ VISA   ☐ MC   ☐ AMEX

Card number _____Exp. Date_____

Card Holder Name_____Card Issue # _____

Signature _____Day Phone_____

☐ **BILL ME:** *(U.S. institutional orders only. Purchase order required.)*

Purchase order # _____
Federal Tax ID 13559302 • GST 89102-8052

Name_____

Address_____

Phone_____ E-mail_____

Copy or detach page and send to: **John Wiley & Sons, One Montgomery Street, Suite 1000, San Francisco, CA 94104-4594**

Order Form can also be faxed to: **888-481-2665**

PROMO JBNND